everyday
potatoes

This is a Parragon book
First published in 2006

Parragon
Queen Street House
4 Queen Street
Bath BA1 1HE, UK

Copyright © Parragon Books Ltd 2006
Designed by Terry Jeavons & Company

ISBN 1-40548-680-5

Printed in China

This book uses imperial and metric measurements. Follow the same units of measurement throughout; do not mix imperial and metric. All spoon measurements are level, unless otherwise stated: teaspoons are assumed to be 5ml, and tablespoons are assumed to be 15ml. Unless otherwise stated, milk is assumed to be whole, eggs and individual fruits such as bananas are medium and pepper is freshly ground black pepper.

Recipes using raw or very lightly cooked eggs should be avoided by infants, the elderly, pregnant women, convalescents and anyone suffering from an illness. Pregnant and breast-feeding women are advised to avoid eating peanuts and peanut products.

everyday
potatoes

introduction

The potato is without doubt one of the most versatile ingredients to have in store. As a nutritional package, potatoes are excellent, containing useful amounts of fibre, minerals such as potassium, and vitamins C and B-complex. Add to this the fact that the scope for making delicious recipes with potatoes as a base is almost unlimited and it will come as no surprise to learn that the potato is one of the world's most popular vegetables, cultivated in almost every country.

Potatoes come in a number of varieties, which lend themselves

to different purposes. Potatoes with a 'waxy' texture are suitable for serving boiled – simply place them in a pan, pour in enough boiling water to cover, put on a lid and boil gently until tender. 'Floury' varieties are ideal for mashing or creaming with butter,

seasoning and a little hot milk, while both waxy and floury varieties can be roasted in oil in the oven until crisp and golden brown. Most varieties can be baked in their skins, which is the best way to preserve their nutritional value – in fact, it is always best to cook potatoes in their skins, then if required, peel them when they are cool enough to handle.

When choosing potatoes, make sure they are firm and well-shaped with a smooth, tight skin. New potatoes should be eaten as fresh as possible – they have a wonderful taste, which is greatly enhanced if you melt butter generously over them – but old potatoes can be stored in a cool, dark place. It is important to keep them away from light, as exposure makes them turn green,

resulting in an unpleasant flavour as well as an increase in the level of naturally occuring toxins, glycoalkaloids.

This book contains a selection of the very best potato recipes from around the world to inspire you to make the most of this humble vegetable.

soups

Potatoes make a perfect base for soups, bringing a smoothness and texture to blended soups and a welcome 'bite' to broths. Their somewhat bland flavour provides a subtle support for other ingredients, allowing their own character to come through.

Soups, like potatoes, seem to lend themselves to every occasion. A light, elegant soup such as Watercress or Broad Bean and Mint makes an attractive starter for a dinner party, while a hearty soup packed with chunks of fish or meat, such as Breton Fish Soup or Chicken and Potato with Bacon, is more than filling enough to serve for lunch or supper, with some fresh crusty bread for dunking. For comfort disguised as soup, you can't beat Leek and Potato Soup, and if you want a taste of Mediterranean sunshine, try Potato and Vegetable Soup with Pistou, a delicious topping bursting with the distinctive taste and aroma of basil.

A few of the recipes in this section are made with sweet potatoes, a distant relative of the potato with a most inviting, deep orange colour and, as the name implies, an appetizing sweetness to the flavour. They work well with the creaminess of blue cheese and the sharpness of apples, and combined with squash and roasted garlic they make a vivid soup to cheer a cold day.

potato & vegetable soup with pesto

ingredients

SERVES 6

2 young carrots

450 g/1 lb potatoes

200 g/7 oz fresh peas
   in the pods

200 g/7 oz French beans

150 g/5^1/$_2$ oz young
   courgettes

2 tbsp olive oil

1 garlic clove, crushed

1 large onion, chopped finely

2.5 litres/4^1/$_2$ pints vegetable
   stock

1 bouquet garni of 2 fresh
   parsley sprigs and 1 bay
   leaf tied in a 7.5-cm/
   3-inch piece of celery

85 g/3 oz dried small soup
   pasta

1 large tomato, skinned,
   deseeded and chopped
   or diced

Parmesan cheese shavings,
   to serve

pesto sauce

75 g/2^3/$_4$ oz fresh basil leaves

1 garlic clove

5 tbsp fruity extra-virgin olive oil

salt and pepper

method

1 To make the pesto sauce, put the basil leaves, garlic and olive oil in a food processor and process until well blended. Season with salt and pepper to taste. Transfer to a bowl, then cover and chill until required.

2 Peel the carrots and cut them in half lengthways, then slice. Peel the potatoes and cut into quarters lengthways, then slice. Set aside.

3 Shell the peas. Top and tail the beans and cut them into 2.5-cm/1-inch pieces. Cut the courgette in half lengthways, then slice.

4 Heat the oil in a large saucepan. Add the garlic and cook for 2 minutes, stirring. Add the onion and continue cooking for 2 minutes, until soft. Add the carrots and potatoes and stir for about 30 seconds.

5 Pour in the stock and bring to the boil. Lower the heat, then partially cover and simmer for 8 minutes, until the vegetables are starting to become tender.

6 Stir in the peas, beans, courgette, bouquet garni, pasta and tomato. Season and cook for about 8–10 minutes, or until tender. Discard the bouquet garni. Stir in the pesto sauce, then serve with Parmesan cheese.

potato & mushroom soup

ingredients

SERVES 4

2 tbsp vegetable oil

600 g/1 lb 5 oz floury
    potatoes, sliced

1 onion, sliced

2 garlic cloves, crushed

1 litre/1³/4 pints beef stock

25 g/1 oz dried mushrooms,
    soaked in hot water for
    20 minutes

2 celery stalks, sliced

2 tbsp brandy

salt and pepper

topping

3 tbsp butter

2 thick slices white bread,
    crusts removed

55 g/2 oz freshly grated
    Parmesan cheese

rehydrated dried mushrooms,
    to garnish

method

1 Heat the vegetable oil in a large frying pan
and add the potato and onion slices and the
garlic. Sauté gently for 5 minutes, stirring
constantly.

2 Add the beef stock, dried mushrooms and
their strained soaking water, and sliced celery.
Bring to the boil, then reduce the heat to a
simmer, cover the pan and cook the soup for
20 minutes, until the potatoes are tender.

3 Meanwhile, melt the butter for the topping in
the frying pan. Sprinkle the bread slices with
the grated cheese and fry the slices in the
butter for 1 minute on each side, until crisp.
Using a sharp knife, cut each slice into
4 triangles.

4 Stir the brandy into the soup, and season
to taste. Pour into warmed bowls and top
with the triangles. Serve garnished with the
rehydrated mushrooms.

leek & potato soup

ingredients

SERVES 4–6

55 g/2 oz butter

1 onion, chopped

3 leeks, sliced

225 g/8 oz potatoes,
    peeled and cut into
    2-cm/³⁄₄-inch cubes

850 ml/1¹⁄₂ pints vegetable
    stock

salt and pepper

150 ml/5 fl oz single cream
    (optional)

2 tbsp snipped fresh chives,
    to garnish

method

1 Melt the butter in a large pan over medium heat, add the prepared vegetables, and sauté gently for 2–3 minutes until soft but not brown. Pour in the stock, bring to the boil, then reduce the heat and simmer, covered, for 15 minutes.

2 Remove from the heat and blend the soup using a stick blender or food processor.

3 Reheat the soup, season with salt and pepper to taste, and serve in warm bowls, swirled with the cream, if using, and garnished with chives.

sweetcorn, potato & cheese soup

ingredients

SERVES 4

55 g/2 oz butter

2 shallots, finely chopped

225 g/8 oz potatoes, peeled
and diced

4 tbsp plain flour

2 tbsp dry white wine

300 ml/10 fl oz milk

325 g/11^{1}/$_{2}$ oz canned corn
kernels, drained

115 g/4 oz grated Swiss
cheese or Cheddar cheese

8–10 fresh sage leaves,
chopped

425 ml/15 fl oz double cream

fresh sage sprigs, to garnish

croûtons

2–3 slices of day-old white
bread

2 tbsp olive oil

method

1 To make the croûtons, cut the crusts off the bread slices, then cut the remaining bread into ^{1}/$_{4}$-inch/5-mm squares. Heat the olive oil in a heavy-based frying pan and add the bread cubes. Cook, tossing and stirring constantly, until evenly coloured. Drain the croûtons thoroughly on kitchen paper and reserve.

2 Melt the butter in a large, heavy-based saucepan. Add the shallots and cook over low heat, stirring occasionally, for 5 minutes or until softened. Add the potatoes and cook, stirring, for 2 minutes.

3 Sprinkle in the flour and cook, stirring, for 1 minute. Remove the pan from the heat and stir in the white wine, then gradually stir in the milk. Return the pan to the heat and bring to the boil, stirring constantly, then reduce the heat and simmer.

4 Stir in the corn kernels, cheese, chopped sage and cream and heat through gently until the cheese has just melted. Ladle the soup into warmed bowls, scatter over the croûtons, garnish with fresh sage sprigs, and serve.

sweet potato & squash soup

ingredients

SERVES 6

350 g/12 oz sweet potatoes

1 acorn squash

4 shallots

olive oil, for brushing

5–6 garlic cloves, unpeeled

850 ml/1½ pints chicken
    stock

125 ml/4 fl oz single cream

salt and pepper

chopped fresh chives,
    to garnish

method

1 Cut the sweet potato, squash, and shallots in half lengthways. Brush the cut sides with oil.

2 Put the vegetables, cut sides down, in a shallow roasting pan. Add the garlic cloves. Roast in a preheated oven, 190°C/375°F for about 40 minutes, until tender and light brown. Remove the pan from the oven and set aside to cool.

3 When cool, scoop the flesh from the potato and squash halves, and put in a saucepan with the shallots. Squeeze out the soft insides from the garlic and add to the other vegetables.

4 Add the stock and a pinch of salt. Bring just to the boil, then reduce the heat and simmer the soup, partially covered, for about 30 minutes, stirring occasionally, until the vegetables are very tender.

5 Let the soup cool slightly, then process until smooth, in batches if necessary, in a blender or food processor. Return the soup to the pan and stir in the cream. Season, then let simmer for 5–10 minutes, until heated through. Garnish with chopped fresh chives and serve immediately.

sweet potato & stilton soup

ingredients

SERVES 4

4 tbsp butter

1 large onion, chopped

2 leeks, trimmed and sliced

175 g/6 oz sweet potatoes,
    peeled and diced

850 ml/1^1/$_2$ pints vegetable
    stock

1 tbsp chopped fresh parsley

1 bay leaf

pepper

150 ml/5 fl oz
    double cream

150 g/5^1/$_2$ oz Stilton cheese,
    crumbled

2 tbsp finely crumbled Stilton
    cheese, to garnish

thick slices of fresh bread,
    to serve

method

1 Melt the butter in a large saucepan over medium heat. Add the onion and leeks and cook, stirring, for about 3 minutes, until slightly softened. Add the sweet potatoes and cook for another 5 minutes, stirring, then pour in the stock, add the parsley and the bay leaf, and season with pepper. Bring to the boil, then lower the heat, cover the pan, and simmer for about 30 minutes. Remove from the heat and let cool for 10 minutes. Remove and discard the bay leaf.

2 Transfer half of the soup into a food processor and blend until smooth. Return to the pan with the rest of the soup, stir in the cream, and cook for another 5 minutes. Gradually stir in the crumbled Stilton until melted (do not let the soup boil).

3 Remove from the heat and ladle into serving bowls. Garnish with finely crumbled Stilton and serve with slices of fresh bread.

sweet potato & apple soup

ingredients

SERVES 6

1 tbsp butter

3 leeks, sliced thinly

1 large carrot, sliced thinly

600 g/1 lb 5 oz sweet
    potatoes, peeled and diced

2 large tart eating apples,
    peeled and diced

1.2 litres/2 pints water

salt and pepper

freshly grated nutmeg

225 ml/8 fl oz apple juice

8 fl oz/225 ml single cream

chopped fresh chives or
    coriander, to garnish

method

1 Melt the butter in a large saucepan over low-medium heat. Add the leeks, then cover and cook, stirring frequently, for 6–8 minutes, or until softened but not coloured.

2 Add the carrot, sweet potatoes, apples, and water. Season lightly with salt, pepper, and nutmeg. Bring to the boil, then reduce the heat, cover and simmer, stirring occasionally, for about 20 minutes, until the vegetables are very tender.

3 Let the soup cool slightly, then transfer to a blender or food processor, and process until smooth, working in batches if necessary.

4 Return the soup to the pan and stir in the apple juice. Place over low heat and simmer for about 10 minutes, until heated through.

5 Stir in the cream and continue simmering for about 5 minutes, stirring frequently, until heated through. Taste and adjust the seasoning, adding more salt, pepper, and nutmeg, if necessary. Ladle the soup into warm bowls, then garnish with a swirl of cream, sprinkle with chives or coriander, and serve.

golden pepper & sweet potato soup

ingredients

SERVES 4

50 g/1³/₄ oz leek (white part only)

50 g/1³/₄ oz celery

90 g/3¹/₄ oz potato, peeled

180 g/6¹/₄ oz sweet potato, peeled

75 g/2³/₄ oz onion, finely chopped

2 cloves garlic, peeled and finely sliced

pinch of ground turmeric

pinch of ground mace

2 bay leaves

850 ml/1¹/₂ pints vegetable stock

90 g/3¹/₄ oz deseeded yellow pepper, roasted, skinned and chopped

1 tbsp sugar

2 tsp lemon juice

flat bread, to serve

for the garnish

1 tsp vegetable oil

40 g/1¹/₂ oz cooked sweetcorn kernels

¹/₂ tsp habanero chilli pepper sauce

method

1 Cut the leek, celery, potato, and sweet potato into ¹/₂-inch/1-cm pieces. Put the onion, garlic, leek, and celery into a large, lidded saucepan over a high heat and cook, stirring constantly, for 5 minutes, or until softened but not coloured.

2 Add the potato, sweet potato, turmeric, mace, bay leaves, and stock, stir well and bring to the boil. Reduce the heat, cover, and let simmer for 20 minutes, or until all the vegetables are soft.

3 Meanwhile, in a separate saucepan, heat the oil, add the corn kernels, and stir-fry until golden brown. Remove from the heat and stir in the chilli sauce. Reserve for garnishing the soup.

4 Remove the bay leaves from the soup and discard. Stir in the roasted pepper, sugar and lemon juice. Using a hand-held electric blender or a food processor, blend the soup until smooth.

5 Ladle into warmed soup bowls, sprinkle with the sweetcorn kernel garnish, and serve with flat bread to accompany.

middle eastern soup with harissa

ingredients

SERVES 6

2 aubergines

3 tbsp olive oil

6 lamb shanks

1 small onion, chopped

400 ml/14 fl oz chicken stock

2 litres/3½ pints water

400 g/14 oz sweet potato,
   cut into chunks

5-cm/2-inch piece
   cinnamon stick

1 tsp ground cumin

2 tbsp chopped fresh
   coriander

hot naan, to serve

for the harissa

2 red peppers, roasted,
   peeled, deseeded
   and chopped

½ tsp coriander seeds,
   dry-fried

25 g/1 oz fresh red chillies,
   chopped

2 garlic cloves, chopped

2 tsp caraway seeds

olive oil

salt

method

1 Prick the aubergines, place on a baking sheet, and bake in a preheated oven, 200°C/400°F, for 1 hour. When cool, peel and chop.

2 Heat the oil in a saucepan. Add the lamb and cook until browned. Add the onion, stock, and water. Bring to the boil. Reduce the heat and let simmer for 1 hour.

3 For the harissa, process the peppers, coriander seeds, chillies, garlic and caraway seeds in a food processor. With the motor running, add enough oil to make a paste. Season, then spoon into a jar. Cover with oil, seal, and let chill.

4 Remove the shanks from the stock, cut off the meat, and chop. Add the sweet potato, cinnamon and cumin to the stock, bring to the boil, cover and let simmer for 20 minutes. Discard the cinnamon and process the mixture in a food processor with the aubergine. Return to the pan, add the lamb and coriander and heat until hot. Serve with the harissa and hot naan.

indian potato & pea soup

ingredients

SERVES 4

2 tbsp vegetable oil

225 g/8 oz diced floury
    potatoes

1 large onion, chopped

2 garlic cloves, crushed

1 tsp garam masala

1 tsp ground coriander

1 tsp ground cumin

850 ml/1$^{1}/_{2}$ pints vegetable
    stock

1 red chilli, seeded
    and chopped

100 g/3$^{1}/_{2}$ oz frozen peas

4 tbsp plain yogurt

salt and pepper

chopped fresh coriander,
    to garnish

warm bread, to serve

method

1 Heat the vegetable oil in a large saucepan and add the diced potatoes, onion, and garlic. Cook over low heat, stirring constantly, for about 5 minutes, until the onion is soft.

2 Add the ground spices and cook for an additional 1 minute, stirring constantly.

3 Stir in the vegetable stock and chopped red chilli and bring to the boil. Reduce the heat, then cover the pan and simmer for 20 minutes, until the potatoes begin to break down.

4 Add the peas and cook for an additional 5 minutes. Stir in the yogurt and season to taste with salt and pepper.

5 Pour into warmed soup bowls. Garnish with chopped fresh coriander and serve immediately with warm bread.

carrot & cumin soup

ingredients

SERVES 4–6

3 tbsp butter or margarine

1 large onion, chopped

1–2 garlic cloves, crushed

350 g/12 oz carrots, sliced

850 ml/1$\frac{1}{2}$ pints chicken or
    vegetable stock

$\frac{3}{4}$ tsp ground cumin

2 celery stalks, sliced thinly

115 g/4 oz potato, diced

2 tsp tomato purée

2 tsp lemon juice

2 fresh or dried bay leaves

300 ml/10 fl oz skim milk

salt and pepper

celery leaves, to garnish

method

1 Melt the butter or margarine in a large saucepan. Add the onion and garlic and cook very gently until softened but not coloured.

2 Add the carrots and cook over low heat for 5 minutes more, stirring frequently and taking care they do not brown.

3 Add the stock, cumin, seasoning, celery, potato, tomato purée, lemon juice, and bay leaves and bring to the boil. Cover and simmer for about 30 minutes, until all the vegetables are tender.

4 Remove and discard the bay leaves, cool the soup a little, and then press it through a sieve, or process in a food processor or blender until smooth.

5 Pour the soup into a clean saucepan, add the milk, and bring to the boil over low heat. Taste and adjust the seasoning if necessary.

6 Ladle into warmed bowls, garnish each serving with a small celery leaf, and serve.

minestrone

ingredients

SERVES 6

2 fresh basil sprigs

2 fresh marjoram sprigs

2 fresh thyme sprigs

2 tbsp olive oil

2 onions, chopped

2 garlic cloves, chopped

4 tomatoes, peeled
   and chopped

125 ml/4 fl oz red wine

1.7 litres/3 pints vegetable
   stock

115 g/4 oz Great Northern
   beans, soaked overnight in
   cold water, then drained

2 carrots, chopped

2 potatoes, chopped

1 small turnip, chopped

1 celery stalk, chopped

1/4 small cabbage, shredded

55 g/2 oz dried stellette or
   other soup pasta shapes

salt and pepper

2 tbsp freshly grated
   Parmesan cheese,
   plus extra for serving

method

1 Chop enough fresh basil, marjoram and thyme to fill 2 tablespoons and reserve until required. Heat the olive oil in a heavy-based saucepan. Add the onions and cook, stirring occasionally, for 5 minutes or until softened. Stir in the garlic and cook for an additional 3 minutes, then stir in the chopped tomatoes and the reserved herbs.

2 Add the wine, simmer for 1–2 minutes, then add the stock and drained beans. Bring to the boil, then reduce the heat, partially cover and simmer for 1 1/2 hours.

3 Add the carrots, potatoes and turnip, then cover and simmer for 15 minutes. Add the celery, cabbage and pasta, then cover and simmer for an additional 10 minutes. Season to taste with salt and pepper and stir in the Parmesan cheese. Ladle into warmed bowls and serve with extra Parmesan cheese.

broad bean & mint soup

ingredients

SERVES 4

2 tbsp olive oil

1 red onion, chopped

2 garlic cloves, crushed

450 g/1 lb diced potatoes

500 g/1 lb 2 oz broad beans,
    thawed if frozen

850 ml/1$\frac{1}{2}$ pints vegetable
    stock

2 tbsp freshly chopped mint

plain yogurt and fresh mint
    sprigs, to garnish

method

1 Heat the olive oil in a large saucepan. Add the onion and garlic and sauté for 2–3 minutes, until softened. Add the potatoes and cook, stirring constantly, for 5 minutes.

2 Stir in the beans and the stock. Cover and simmer gently for 30 minutes or until the beans and potatoes are tender.

3 Remove a few vegetables with a slotted spoon and set aside. Place the remainder of the soup in a food processor or blender and process to a smooth purée.

4 Return the soup to a clean saucepan and add the reserved vegetables and chopped mint. Stir thoroughly and heat through gently.

5 Ladle the soup into individual serving bowls. Garnish with swirls of plain yogurt and sprigs of fresh mint and serve immediately.

watercress soup

ingredients

SERVES 4

2 bunches of watercress
    (approx 200 g/7 oz),
    thoroughly cleaned

3 tbsp butter

2 onions, chopped

225 g/8 oz potatoes, peeled
    and roughly chopped

1.2 litres/2 pints vegetable
    stock or water

salt and pepper

whole nutmeg, for grating

125 ml/4 fl oz crème fraîche,
    yogurt, or sour cream

method

1 Remove the leaves from the watercress stalks and set aside. Coarsely chop the stalks.

2 Melt the butter in a large saucepan over medium heat, add the onion and cook for 4–5 minutes until soft. Do not brown.

3 Add the potato to the pan and mix well with the onion. Add the watercress stalks and the stock. Bring to the boil, then reduce the heat, cover, and simmer for 15–20 minutes until the potato is soft.

4 Add the watercress leaves and stir in to heat through. Remove from the heat and use a hand-held stick blender to process the soup until smooth. Alternatively, pour the soup into a blender, process until smooth, and return to the rinsed-out pan. Reheat and season with salt and pepper to taste, adding a good grating of nutmeg, if using.

5 Serve in warm bowls with the crème fraîche spooned on top.

lentil, potato & ham soup

ingredients

SERVES 5

300 g/10½ oz Puy lentils

2 tsp butter

1 large onion, chopped finely

2 carrots, chopped finely

1 garlic clove, chopped finely

2 cups water

1 bay leaf

¼ tsp dried sage or rosemary

450 ml/16 fl oz chicken stock

225 g/8 oz finely diced
    potatoes

1 tbsp tomato purée

115 g/4 oz finely diced
    smoked ham

salt and pepper

chopped fresh parsley,
    to garnish

method

1 Rinse the lentils under cold running water, then drain and pick over to check for any small stones.

2 Melt the butter in a large saucepan or flameproof casserole over medium heat. Add the onion, carrots and garlic, then cover and cook, stirring frequently, for 4–5 minutes, until the onion is slightly softened but not coloured.

3 Add the lentils to the vegetables with the measured water, bay leaf and sage or rosemary. Bring to the boil, then reduce the heat, cover, and simmer for 10 minutes.

4 Add the stock, potatoes, tomato purée and ham. Bring back to a simmer. Cover and continue simmering for 25–30 minutes, or until the vegetables are tender.

5 Season to taste with salt and pepper and remove the bay leaf. Ladle into warm bowls, then garnish with parsley and serve.

chicken & potato soup with bacon

ingredients

SERVES 4

1 tbsp butter

2 garlic cloves, chopped

1 onion, sliced

250 g/9 oz smoked lean
bacon, chopped

2 large leeks, trimmed
and sliced

2 tbsp plain flour

1 litre/1¾ pints chicken stock

800 g/1 lb 12 oz potatoes,
peeled and chopped

200 g/7 oz skinless chicken
breast, chopped

salt and pepper

4 tbsp double cream

grilled bacon, chopped,
to garnish

fresh crusty rolls, to serve

method

1 Melt the butter in a large saucepan over medium heat. Add the garlic and onion and cook, stirring, for 3 minutes, until slightly softened. Add the chopped bacon and leeks and cook for another 3 minutes, stirring.

2 In a bowl, mix the flour with enough stock to make a smooth paste and stir it into the pan. Cook, stirring, for 2 minutes. Pour in the remaining stock, then add the potatoes and chicken. Season with salt and pepper. Bring to the boil, then lower the heat and simmer for 25 minutes, until the chicken and potatoes are tender and cooked through.

3 Stir in the cream and cook for 2 minutes more, then remove from the heat and ladle into serving bowls. Garnish the soup with chopped bacon and serve with fresh crusty rolls.

smoked cod chowder

ingredients

SERVES 4

2 tbsp butter

1 onion, finely chopped

1 small celery stalk,
    finely diced

250 g/9 oz potatoes, diced

55 g/2 oz carrots, diced

300 ml/10 fl oz boiling water

350 g/12 oz smoked cod
    fillets, skinned and cut
    into bite-size pieces

300 ml/10 fl oz milk

salt and pepper

method

1 Melt the butter in a large saucepan over low heat, add the onion and celery, and cook, stirring frequently, for 5 minutes or until softened but not browned.

2 Add the potatoes, carrots and water to the pan, and season to taste with salt and pepper. Bring to the boil, then reduce the heat and let simmer for 10 minutes, or until the vegetables are tender. Add the fish to the chowder and cook for an additional 10 minutes.

3 Pour in the milk and heat gently. Taste and adjust the seasoning, if necessary. Serve hot.

cod & sweet potato soup

ingredients

SERVES 4

4 tbsp lemon juice

1 fresh red chilli, seeded
and finely sliced

pinch of nutmeg

250 g/9 oz cod fillets,
skinned, rinsed, and dried

1 tbsp vegetable oil

1 onion, chopped

4 spring onions, chopped

2 garlic cloves, chopped

450 g/1 lb sweet potatoes,
diced

1 litre/1³/4 pints vegetable
stock

salt and pepper

1 carrot, sliced

150 g/5¹/2 oz white cabbage,
shredded

2 celery stalks, sliced

crusty bread, to serve

method

1 Put the lemon juice, chilli and nutmeg in a
shallow, non-metallic dish and mix together.
Cut the cod into chunks and add to the dish.
Turn in the marinade until well coated. Cover
with clingfilm and leave to marinate in the
refrigerator for 30 minutes.

2 Heat the oil in a large saucepan over
medium heat. Add the onion and spring
onions and cook, stirring frequently, for 4
minutes. Add the garlic and cook, stirring, for
2 minutes.

3 Add the sweet potatoes, stock, and salt and
pepper to taste. Bring to the boil, then reduce
the heat, cover, and let simmer for 10 minutes.
Add the carrot, cabbage and celery, season
again, and simmer for 8–10 minutes.

4 Let the soup cool slightly, then transfer to a
blender or food processor and process until
smooth, working in batches if necessary.
Return to the pan. Add the fish and marinade
and bring gently to the boil. Reduce the heat
and let simmer for 10 minutes. Ladle the
soup into bowls and serve with crusty bread.

breton fish soup with cider & sorrel

ingredients

SERVES 4

2 tsp butter

1 large leek, thinly sliced

2 shallots, finely chopped

125 ml/4 fl oz dry cider

300 ml/10 fl oz fish stock

250 g/9 oz potatoes, diced

1 bay leaf

4 tbsp plain flour

200 ml/7 fl oz milk

200 ml/7 fl oz double cream

55 g/2 oz sorrel leaves

350 g/12 oz skinless angler
    fish or cod fillets, cut into
    1-inch/2.5-cm pieces

salt and pepper

method

1 Melt the butter in a large saucepan over low-medium heat. Add the leek and shallots, and cook, stirring frequently, for 5 minutes or until they start to soften. Add the cider and bring to the boil.

2 Stir in the stock, potatoes and bay leaf with a large pinch of salt (unless the stock is salty) and return to the boil. Reduce the heat, cover, and cook gently for 10 minutes.

3 Put the flour in a small bowl and very slowly whisk in a few tablespoons of the milk to make a thick paste. Stir in a little more milk to make a smooth liquid. Adjust the heat so that the soup bubbles gently. Stir in the flour mixture and cook, stirring frequently, for 5 minutes. Add the remaining milk and half the cream. Cook for an additional 10 minutes or until the potatoes are tender.

4 Finely chop the sorrel and combine with the remaining cream. Stir into the soup and add the fish. Cook, stirring occasionally, for an additional 3 minutes or until the monkfish stiffens or the cod just begins to flake. Taste the soup and adjust the seasoning, if necessary. Ladle into warmed bowls and serve.

bouillabaisse

ingredients

SERVES 6

450 g/1 lb king prawns
750 g/1 lb 10 oz firm white
    fish fillets
4 tbsp olive oil
grated rind of 1 orange
1 large garlic clove,
    chopped finely
$1/2$ tsp chilli paste or harissa
1 large leek, sliced
1 onion, halved and sliced
1 red pepper, seeded
    and sliced
4 tomatoes, cored and
    cut into 8
4 garlic cloves, sliced
1 bay leaf
pinch of saffron threads
$1/2$ tsp fennel seeds
600 ml/1 pint water
1.2 litres/2 pints
    fish stock
1 fennel bulb, chopped finely
1 large onion, chopped finely
225 g/8 oz potatoes, halved
    and sliced thinly
250 g/9 oz scallops
salt and pepper

to serve

ready-made aïoli
toasted French bread slices
dill sprigs, to garnish

method

1 Peel the prawns and reserve the shells. Cut the fish into pieces 2 inches/5 cm square. Trim any ragged edges and reserve. Put the fish in a bowl with 2 tablespoons of the olive oil, the orange rind, crushed garlic, and chilli paste or harissa. Turn to coat, cover and chill the prawns and fish separately in the refrigerator.

2 Heat 1 tablespoon of the olive oil in a large saucepan over medium heat. Add the leek, onion, and red pepper. Cook, stirring frequently, for 5 minutes, until the onion softens. Stir in the tomatoes, sliced garlic, bay leaf, saffron, fennel seeds, prawn shells, water and fish stock. Bring to the boil, reduce the heat and simmer, covered, for 30 minutes. Strain well.

3 Heat the remaining oil in a large saucepan. Add the fennel and onion and cook, stirring frequently, until the onion softens. Add the stock and potatoes and bring to the boil. Reduce the heat slightly, cover and cook for 12–15 minutes, or until the potatoes are just tender. Reduce the heat to a simmer and add the fish, starting with the thicker pieces and adding the thinner ones after 2–3 minutes. Add the prawns and scallops and simmer until all the fish is cooked and opaque.

4 Spread the aïoli on the toasted bread slices and arrange on top of the soup. Garnish with dill sprigs and serve immediately.

haddock & potato soup

ingredients

SERVES 4

2 tbsp butter

1 onion, chopped

1 leek, chopped

2 tbsp plain flour

850 ml/1^{1}/$_{2}$ pints milk

1 bay leaf

2 tbsp chopped fresh parsley,
    plus extra to garnish

salt and pepper

350 g/12 oz smoked haddock
    fillets, skinned

450 g/1 lb potatoes,
    cooked and mashed

6 tbsp double cream

crusty rolls, to serve

green salad, to serve

method

1 Melt the butter in a large saucepan over medium heat, add the onion and leek and cook, stirring frequently, for 3 minutes, or until slightly softened. Mix the flour in a bowl with enough of the milk to make a smooth paste, then stir into the pan. Cook, stirring constantly, for 2 minutes, then gradually stir in the remaining milk. Add the bay leaf and parsley and season to taste with salt and pepper. Bring to the boil, then reduce the heat and simmer for 15 minutes.

2 Rinse the haddock fillets under cold running water, drain, then cut into bite-size chunks. Add to the soup and cook for 15 minutes, or until the fish is tender and cooked right through. Add the mashed potatoes and stir in the cream. Cook for a further 2–3 minutes, then remove from the heat and remove and discard the bay leaf.

3 Ladle into warmed serving bowls, garnish with chopped parsley, and serve with crusty rolls and a green salad.

quick clam chowder

ingredients

SERVES 4

2 tsp corn oil

115 g/4 oz rindless lean
    bacon, diced

2 tbsp butter

1 onion, chopped

2 celery stalks, chopped

2 potatoes, chopped

salt and pepper

2 leeks, sliced

400 g/14 oz canned chopped
    tomatoes

3 tbsp chopped fresh parsley

1.2 litres/2 pints fish stock

550 g/1 lb 4 oz canned clams,
    drained and rinsed

method

1 Heat the oil in a heavy-based saucepan.
Add the bacon and cook over medium heat,
stirring, for 5 minutes or until the fat runs and
it begins to crisp. Remove from the pan, drain
on kitchen paper and reserve.

2 Melt the butter in the pan. Add the onion,
celery and potatoes with a pinch of salt.
Cover and cook over low heat, stirring
occasionally, for 10 minutes, or until soft.

3 Stir in the leeks, the tomatoes and their
juices, and 2 tablespoons of the parsley. Pour
in the stock, bring to the boil, reduce the heat
and simmer for 10–15 minutes, or until the
vegetables are tender. Season to taste with
salt and pepper and stir in the clams.

4 Heat the soup gently for 2–3 minutes, then
ladle into warmed bowls, garnish with the
remaining parsley and reserved bacon,
and serve.

salads

Potato salads are popular the world over, and this chapter introduces you to a selection of the best. Hot potatoes are delicious, but served at room temperature or chilled they take on a completely different flavour, much more intense and really quite gorgeous, and a firm texture that works very well with dressings.

A real classic in the range of potato salads is the French Tuna Niçoise Salad, a mouthwatering combination of tiny new potatoes, French beans, hard-boiled eggs, crisp lettuce, juicy tomatoes, olives and anchovies, the whole lot topped with tuna – a fresh tuna steak is best, but canned tuna makes an excellent substitute. A variation of this is Russian Salad, confusingly served in Spanish tapas bars! This version has cooked carrots and peas as well as French beans, and also includes sliced gherkins.

Floury potatoes marry well with Indian spices in a yogurt dressing, the softer texture of the potato absorbing the flavours readily. The cool, sweet flesh of fresh mango counteracts the heat of an Indian Potato Salad and crisp, just-cooked broccoli adds colour and texture.

For an impressive summer lunch-party dish, try Nests of Chinese Salad – the 'nests' are made of grated potatoes shaped in two sieves and deep-fried until irresistibly crisp.

potato salad

ingredients

SERVES 4

700 g/1 lb 9 oz tiny
    new potatoes
8 spring onions
1 hard-boiled egg (optional)
250 ml/9 fl oz low-fat
    mayonnaise
1 tsp paprika
salt and pepper
2 tbsp chopped fresh chives
pinch of paprika, to garnish

method

1 Bring a large saucepan of lightly salted water to the boil. Add the potatoes to the pan and cook for about 10–15 minutes, or until they are just tender. Drain the potatoes in a colander and rinse them under cold running water until they are completely cold. Drain them again thoroughly. Transfer the potatoes to a mixing bowl and set aside.

2 Trim and slice the spring onions thinly on the diagonal. Chop the hard-boiled egg, if using.

3 Combine the mayonnaise, paprika and salt and pepper to taste in a bowl until well blended. Pour the mixture over the potatoes. Add the sliced spring onions and chopped egg, if using, and toss together.

4 Transfer the potato salad to a serving bowl. Sprinkle with chopped chives and a pinch of paprika. Cover and chill in the refrigerator until ready to serve.

indian potato salad

ingredients

SERVES 4

900 g/2 lb diced floury
   potatoes
75 g/2³/₄ oz small broccoli
   florets
1 small mango, diced
4 spring onions, sliced
salt and pepper
small cooked spiced
   poppadoms, to serve

dressing

¹/₂ tsp ground cumin
¹/₂ tsp ground coriander
1 tbsp mango chutney
150 ml/5 fl oz low-fat plain
   yogurt
1 tsp chopped fresh root
   ginger
2 tbsp chopped fresh
   coriander

method

1 Cook the potatoes in a large saucepan of
boiling water for 10 minutes, or until tender.
Drain well and place in a mixing bowl.

2 Meanwhile, blanch the broccoli florets
in a separate saucepan of boiling water for
2 minutes. Drain the broccoli well and add to
the potatoes in the bowl.

3 When the potatoes and broccoli have cooled,
add the diced mango and sliced spring
onions. Season to taste with salt and pepper
and mix well to combine.

4 In a small bowl, stir the dressing ingredients
together. Spoon the dressing over the potato
mixture and mix together carefully, taking care
not to break up the potatoes and broccoli.

5 Serve the salad immediately, accompanied
by the small cooked spiced poppadoms.

nests of chinese salad

ingredients

SERVES 4

potato nests

450 g/1 lb grated floury
    potatoes
125 g/4^{1}/$_{2}$ oz cornflour
vegetable oil, for deep-frying
fresh chives, to garnish

salad

125 g/4^{1}/$_{2}$ oz pineapple, diced
1 green pepper, deseeded
    and cut into strips
1 carrot, cut into thin strips
50 g/1^{3}/$_{4}$ oz mangetout,
    sliced thickly
4 baby corn cobs,
    halved lengthways
25 g/1 oz bean sprouts
2 spring onions, sliced

dressing

1 tbsp honey
1 tsp light soy sauce
1 garlic clove, crushed
1 tsp lemon juice

method

1 To make the nests, rinse the potatoes several times in cold water. Drain well on kitchen paper so that they are completely dry. This is to prevent the potatoes from spitting when they are cooked in the oil. Place the potatoes in a large mixing bowl. Add the cornflour, mixing well to coat the potatoes.

2 Half fill a wok with vegetable oil and heat until smoking. Line a 15-cm/6-inch diameter wire sieve with a quarter of the potato mixture and press another sieve of the same size on top.

3 Lower the sieves into the oil and cook for 2 minutes, until the potato nest is golden brown and crisp. Remove from the wok, and drain well on kitchen paper. Repeat 3 more times, to use up all of the mixture and make a total of 4 nests. Set aside to cool.

4 Combine all the salad ingredients, then spoon the salad into the potato baskets. Combine the dressing ingredients. Pour the dressing over the salad. Garnish with fresh chives and then serve immediately.

herby potato salad

ingredients

SERVES 4

500 g/1 lb 2 oz new potatoes

salt and pepper

16 vine-ripened cherry
　tomatoes, halved

55 g/2 oz black olives, pitted
　and roughly chopped

4 spring onions, finely sliced

2 tbsp chopped fresh mint

2 tbsp chopped fresh parsley

2 tbsp chopped fresh
　coriander

juice of 1 lemon

3 tbsp extra-virgin olive oil

method

1 Cook the potatoes in a saucepan of lightly salted boiling water for 15 minutes, or until tender. Drain, then cool slightly before peeling off the skins. Cut into halves or quarters, depending on the size of the potato. Then combine with the tomatoes, olives, spring onions and herbs in a salad bowl.

2 Mix the lemon juice and oil together in a small bowl or jug and pour over the potato salad. Season to taste with salt and pepper before serving.

grilled new potato salad

ingredients

SERVES 4

675 g/1 lb 8 oz new
    potatoes, scrubbed

3 tbsp olive oil

2 tbsp chopped fresh thyme

1 tsp paprika

4 smoked bacon strips

salt and pepper

fresh parsley sprig, to garnish

dressing

4 tbsp mayonnaise

1 tbsp garlic wine vinegar

2 garlic cloves, crushed

1 tbsp chopped fresh parsley

method

1 Cook the new potatoes in a large saucepan of boiling water for about 10 minutes, until tender. Drain well and turn into a bowl.

2 Combine the olive oil, chopped thyme and paprika, and pour the mixture over the warm potatoes, tossing gently to coat.

3 Place the bacon strips under a preheated medium grill and cook, turning once, for 5 minutes, until crisp. When cooked, roughly chop the bacon and keep warm.

4 Transfer the potatoes to the grill pan and cook for 10 minutes, turning once.

5 Combine the dressing ingredients in a small serving bowl. Transfer the potatoes and bacon to a large serving bowl. Season to taste with salt and pepper and mix together thoroughly.

6 Spoon over the dressing. Garnish with a parsley sprig and serve immediately for a warm salad. Alternatively, cool and serve chilled.

sweet potato salad

ingredients

SERVES 4

500 g/1 lb 2 oz diced sweet
  potatoes

4 tbsp butter

1 tbsp lemon juice

1 garlic clove, crushed

1 red pepper, deseeded
  and diced

1 green pepper, deseeded
  and diced

2 bananas, peeled and sliced
  thickly

2 thick slices white bread,
  crusts removed, diced

salt and pepper

dressing

2 tbsp honey

2 tbsp chopped fresh chives

2 tbsp lemon juice

2 tbsp olive oil

method

1 Cook the sweet potatoes in a large saucepan of boiling water for 10–15 minutes, until tender. Drain thoroughly and set aside.

2 Meanwhile, melt the butter in a frying pan. Add the lemon juice, garlic and peppers and cook, stirring constantly, for 3 minutes. Add the bananas and cook for 1 minute. Remove the mixture from the pan with a slotted spoon and stir into the potatoes.

3 Add the bread cubes to the frying pan and cook, stirring frequently, for 2 minutes, until they are golden brown on all sides.

4 Mix the dressing ingredients together in a small bowl and heat until well combined.

5 Spoon the potato mixture into a serving dish and season to taste with salt and pepper. Pour the dressing over the potatoes and sprinkle the croûtons over the top. Serve the sweet potato salad immediately.

potato, rocket & apple salad

ingredients

SERVES 4

600 g/1 lb 5 oz potatoes,
    unpeeled and sliced
2 green eating apples,
    cored and diced
1 tsp lemon juice
25 g/1 oz walnut pieces
125 g/4^1/$_2$ oz goat's cheese,
    diced
150 g/5^1/$_2$ oz rocket leaves
salt and pepper

dressing

2 tbsp olive oil
1 tbsp red wine vinegar
1 tsp honey
1 tsp fennel seeds

method

1 Cook the potatoes in a saucepan of boiling water for 15 minutes, until tender. Drain thoroughly and cool. Transfer the cooled potatoes to a serving bowl.

2 Toss the diced apples in the lemon juice, then drain, and stir them into the potatoes. Add the walnut pieces, cheese cubes, and rocket leaves, then toss the salad to mix. Season to taste.

3 In a small bowl or jug, whisk the dressing ingredients together and then pour the dressing over the salad. Serve immediately.

mixed vegetable salad

ingredients

SERVES 4

450 g/1 lb waxy new
    potatoes, scrubbed
1 carrot, cut into thin sticks
225 g/8 oz cauliflower florets
225 g/8 oz baby corn cobs,
    halved lengthways
175 g/6 oz French beans
175 g/6 oz diced ham
50 g/1³/₄ oz mushrooms,
    sliced
salt and pepper

dressing

2 tbsp chopped fresh parsley
150 ml/5 fl oz mayonnaise
150 ml/5 fl oz plain yogurt
4 tsp lemon juice
grated rind of 1 lemon
2 tsp fennel seeds

method

1 Cook the potatoes in a large saucepan of
boiling water for 15 minutes, or until tender.
Drain thoroughly and cool. When the potatoes
are cold, slice them thinly.

2 Cook the carrot sticks, cauliflower florets,
baby corn cobs and French beans in a
saucepan of boiling water for 5 minutes. Drain
and cool.

3 Reserving 1 teaspoon of the chopped
parsley for the garnish, combine the remaining
dressing ingredients in a bowl.

4 Arrange the vegetables on a salad platter
and top with the diced ham and sliced
mushrooms. Spoon the dressing over the
salad and garnish with the reserved parsley.
Serve immediately.

radish & cucumber salad

ingredients

SERVES 4

500 g/1 lb 2 oz new potatoes,
    scrubbed and halved
1/2 cucumber, sliced thinly
2 tsp salt
1 bunch of radishes,
    sliced thinly

dressing

1 tbsp Dijon mustard
2 tbsp olive oil
1 tbsp white wine vinegar
2 tbsp chopped mixed herbs

method

1 Cook the potatoes in a saucepan of boiling water for 10–15 minutes, or until tender. Drain thoroughly and set aside to cool.

2 Meanwhile, spread out the cucumber slices on a plate and sprinkle with the salt. Set aside for 30 minutes, then rinse well under cold running water, and pat thoroughly dry with kitchen paper.

3 Arrange the cucumber and radish slices on a serving plate in a decorative pattern and pile the cooked potatoes in the centre of the slices.

4 In a small bowl, combine all the dressing ingredients, whisking until thoroughly mixed. Pour the dressing over the salad, tossing well to coat all of the ingredients. Chill in the refrigerator before serving.

beetroot salad & dill dressing

ingredients

SERVES 4

450 g/1 lb diced waxy
    potatoes

4 small cooked beetroot,
    sliced

$\frac{1}{2}$ small cucumber, sliced thinly

2 large dill pickles, sliced

1 red onion, halved and sliced

fresh dill sprigs, to garnish

dressing

1 garlic clove, crushed

2 tbsp olive oil

2 tbsp red wine vinegar

2 tbsp chopped fresh dill

salt and pepper

method

1 Cook the potatoes in a saucepan of boiling water for 15 minutes, or until tender. Drain and set aside to cool. When cool, combine the potato and sliced beetroot in a large bowl and set aside.

2 Line a large salad platter with the slices of cucumber, dill pickles and red onion. Carefully spoon the potato and beetroot mixture into the centre of the platter.

3 In a small bowl, whisk together all the dressing ingredients, then pour over the salad.

4 Serve the potato and beetroot salad immediately, garnished with fresh dill sprigs.

italian sausage salad

ingredients

SERVES 4

450 g/1 lb waxy potatoes

1 radicchio or lollo rosso lettuce

1 green pepper, deseeded
    and sliced

175 g/6 oz Italian sausage,
    sliced

1 red onion, halved and sliced

125 g/4^1/$_2$ oz sun-dried
    tomatoes in oil, drained
    and sliced

2 tbsp shredded fresh basil

dressing

1 tbsp balsamic vinegar

1 tsp tomato purée

2 tbsp olive oil

salt and pepper

method

1 Cook the potatoes in a large saucepan of boiling water for about 20 minutes, or until cooked through. Drain and cool.

2 Separate the radicchio leaves or lollo rosso lettuce leaves. Line a large serving platter with the leaves.

3 Slice the cooled potatoes and arrange them in layers on the leaf-lined platter together with the sliced green pepper, sliced Italian sausage, red onion and sun-dried tomatoes. Sprinkle with the shredded fresh basil.

4 In a small bowl, whisk the balsamic vinegar, tomato purée and olive oil together and season to taste with salt and pepper. Pour the dressing over the potato salad and serve immediately.

indonesian chicken salad

ingredients

SERVES 4

1.25 kg/2 lb 12 oz waxy
   potatoes, cut into
   small dice

300 g/10^1/$_2$ oz fresh pineapple,
   peeled and diced

2 carrots, grated

175 g/6 oz bean sprouts

1 bunch of spring onions,
   sliced

1 large courgette,
   cut into thin sticks

3 celery stalks,
   cut into thin sticks

175 g/6 oz unsalted peanuts

2 cooked skinless, boneless
   chicken breast portions,
   about 125 g/4^1/$_2$ oz each,
   sliced

dressing

6 tbsp crunchy peanut butter

6 tbsp olive oil

2 tbsp light soy sauce

1 fresh red chilli, deseeded
   and chopped

2 tsp sesame oil

4 tsp lime juice

method

1 Cook the diced potatoes in a saucepan of boiling water for about 10 minutes, or until tender. Drain them thoroughly in a colander and cool, then transfer to a salad bowl.

2 Add the diced pineapple, grated carrots, bean sprouts, spring onions, courgette and celery sticks, peanuts and sliced chicken to the bowl of potatoes. Toss thoroughly to mix all the salad ingredients together.

3 To make the dressing, put the peanut butter in a small mixing bowl and gradually whisk in the olive oil and light soy sauce with a fork or a balloon whisk. Stir in the chilli, sesame oil and lime juice. Mix well until combined.

4 Pour the spicy dressing over the salad and toss lightly to coat all of the ingredients. Serve the potato and chicken salad immediately.

spicy chicken salad

ingredients

SERVES 4

2 skinless, boneless chicken
    breast portions, about
    125 g/4^1/$_2$ oz each

2 tbsp butter

1 fresh red chilli, deseeded
    and chopped

1 tbsp honey

^{1}/$_2$ tsp ground cumin

2 tbsp chopped fresh
    coriander

600 g/1 lb 5 oz diced
    potatoes

50 g/1^3/$_4$ oz French beans,
    halved

1 red pepper, deseeded
    and cut into thin strips

2 tomatoes, deseeded and
    diced

dressing

2 tbsp olive oil

pinch of chilli powder

1 tbsp garlic wine vinegar

pinch of caster sugar

1 tbsp chopped fresh
    coriander

method

1 Cut the chicken into thin strips. Melt the
butter in a heavy saucepan and add the
chicken strips, fresh red chilli, honey and
cumin. Cook for 10 minutes, turning until
cooked through. Transfer the mixture to a bowl
and cool, then stir in the chopped coriander.

2 Meanwhile, cook the diced potatoes in a
saucepan of boiling water for 10 minutes, until
they are tender. Drain and cool.

3 Blanch the French beans in a saucepan of
boiling water for 3 minutes. Drain well and
leave to cool. Combine the French beans and
potatoes in a mixing bowl. Add the pepper
strips and tomatoes to the potato mixture. Stir
in the chicken mixture.

4 In a small bowl, whisk the dressing
ingredients together and pour the dressing
over the salad, tossing well. Transfer the spicy
chicken salad to a serving bowl or large platter
and serve immediately.

russian salad

ingredients

SERVES 2

2 eggs

450 g/1 lb baby new
   potatoes, quartered

115 g/4 oz fine French beans,
   cut into 2.5-cm/
   1-inch lengths

115 g/4 oz frozen peas

115 g/4 oz carrots, cut into
   julienne strips about
   1 inch/2.5 cm in length

200 g/7 oz canned tuna steak
   in olive oil, drained and
   flaked into large chunks

2 tbsp lemon juice

8 tbsp mayonnaise

1 garlic clove, crushed

salt and pepper

4 small gherkins, sliced

8 pitted black olives, halved

1 tbsp capers

1 tbsp chopped fresh
   flatleaf parsley

1 tbsp chopped fresh dill,
   plus extra sprigs to garnish

method

1 Put the eggs in a saucepan, cover with cold water, and slowly bring to the boil. Immediately reduce the heat to very low, cover and simmer gently for 10 minutes. Drain and immediately put under cold running water to prevent a black ring from forming round the egg yolk. Gently tap the eggs to crack the eggshells and set aside until cold.

2 Meanwhile, bring the potatoes to the boil in a large saucepan of cold, salted water. Lower the heat and simmer for 7 minutes, or until just tender. Add the beans and peas to the pan for the last 2 minutes of cooking. Drain well, splash under cold running water, then cool completely. Transfer to a large bowl.

3 Add the carrot strips and the flaked tuna and very gently toss the ingredients together. Transfer the vegetables and tuna to a salad bowl or large serving dish.

4 In a jug, stir the lemon juice into the mayonnaise, then stir in the garlic and season to taste with salt and pepper. Drizzle the dressing over the vegetables and tuna.

5 Sprinkle the gherkins, olives and capers into the salad and finally sprinkle over the parsley and dill. Just before serving, shell the eggs, then slice them into wedges, add them to the salad and garnish with dill sprigs. Serve at room temperature.

tuna niçoise salad

ingredients

SERVES 4

4 eggs

450 g/1 lb new potatoes

115 g/4 oz French beans,
trimmed and halved

2 x 175 g/6 oz tuna steaks

6 tbsp olive oil, plus extra
for brushing

1 garlic clove, crushed

1 1/2 tsp Dijon mustard

2 tsp lemon juice

2 tbsp chopped fresh basil

salt and pepper

2 little gem lettuces

200 g/7 oz cherry tomatoes,
halved

175 g/6 oz cucumber, peeled,
halved and sliced

50 g/1 3/4 oz pitted black
olives

50 g/1 3/4 oz canned
anchovies in oil, drained

method

1 Bring a small saucepan of water to the boil. Add the eggs and cook for 7–9 minutes from when the water returns to the boil: 7 minutes for a slightly soft centre, 9 minutes for a firm centre. Drain and refresh under cold running water. Set aside.

2 Cook the potatoes in boiling salted water for 10–12 minutes, until tender. Add the beans 3 minutes before the end of the cooking time. Drain both vegetables well and refresh under cold water. Drain well.

3 Wash and dry the tuna steaks. Brush with a little olive oil and season. Cook on a preheated ridged griddle pan for 2–3 minutes each side, until just tender but still slightly pink in the centre. Set aside to rest.

4 Whisk together the garlic, mustard, lemon juice, basil and seasoning to taste. Whisk in the olive oil.

5 To assemble the salad, break apart the lettuces and tear into large pieces. Divide among individual serving plates. Next add the potatoes and beans, tomatoes, cucumber and olives. Toss lightly together. Shell the eggs and quarter lengthways, then arrange on top of the salad. Sprinkle over the anchovies. Flake the tuna steaks and arrange on the salads. Pour over the dressing and serve.

tuna, egg & potato salad

ingredients

SERVES 4

350 g/12 oz new potatoes,
    unpeeled

1 hard-boiled egg,
    cooled and shelled

3 tbsp olive oil

1$\frac{1}{2}$ tbsp white wine vinegar

salt and pepper

115 g/4 oz canned tuna in oil,
    drained and flaked

2 shallots, finely chopped

1 tomato, peeled and diced

2 tbsp chopped fresh parsley

method

1 Cook the potatoes in a saucepan of lightly salted boiling water for 10 minutes, then remove from the heat, cover and stand for 15–20 minutes, or until tender. Drain, then peel and thinly slice.

2 Meanwhile, slice the egg, then cut each slice in half. Whisk the olive oil and vinegar together in a bowl and season to taste with salt and pepper. Spoon a little of the vinaigrette into a serving dish to coat the base.

3 Place half the potato slices over the base of the dish and season to taste with salt, then top with half the flaked tuna, half the egg slices and half the shallots. Pour over half the remaining dressing. Make a second layer with the remaining potato slices, tuna, egg and shallots. Pour over the remaining dressing.

4 Finally, top the salad with the tomato and parsley. Cover with clingfilm and stand in a cool place for 1–2 hours before serving.

mackerel & potato salad

ingredients

SERVES 4

125 g/4¹/₂ oz new potatoes,
   scrubbed and diced
225 g/8 oz mackerel fillets,
   skinned
1.2 litres/2 pints water
1 bay leaf
1 slice of lemon
1 eating apple, cored and diced
1 shallot, thinly sliced
3 tbsp white wine vinegar
1 tsp sunflower oil
1¹/₂ tsp caster sugar
¹/₄ tsp Dijon mustard
salt and pepper

to serve

2 tbsp low-fat plain yogurt
¹/₄ cucumber, thinly sliced
1 bunch of watercress
1 tbsp snipped fresh chives

method

1 Steam the potatoes over a saucepan of simmering water for 10 minutes, or until tender.

2 Meanwhile, cut the mackerel into bite-size pieces. Bring the water to the boil in a large, shallow saucepan, then reduce the heat so that it is just simmering and add the fish pieces, bay leaf and lemon. Poach for 3 minutes, or until the flesh of the fish is opaque. Remove with a slotted spoon and transfer to a serving dish.

3 Drain the potatoes and transfer to a large bowl. Add the apple and shallot and mix well, then spoon the mixture over the fish.

4 Mix the vinegar, oil, sugar and mustard together in a jug, season to taste with salt and pepper, and whisk thoroughly. Pour the dressing over the potato mixture. Cover and chill in the refrigerator for up to 6 hours.

5 To serve, spread the yogurt over the salad, then arrange the cucumber decoratively on top. Add sprigs of watercress and sprinkle with the chives.

soused trout & potato salad

ingredients

SERVES 4

4 trout, about 225–350 g/
    8–12 oz each, filleted,
    trimmed and skinned
1 onion, very thinly sliced
2 bay leaves
fresh parsley and dill sprigs,
    or other fresh herbs
10–12 black peppercorns
4–6 cloves
salt
150 ml/5 fl oz red wine
    vinegar
salad leaves, to garnish

potato salad
500 g/1 lb 2 oz small
    new potatoes
2 tbsp French dressing
4 tbsp thick mayonnaise
3–4 spring onions, sliced

method

1 Lightly grease a shallow ovenproof dish and lay the trout fillets in it, packing them fairly tightly together but keeping them in a single layer. Arrange the sliced onion, bay leaves and herbs over the fish.

2 Put the peppercorns, cloves, salt and vinegar into a saucepan and bring almost to the boil. Remove from the heat and pour evenly over the fish. Leave to cool, then cover, and marinate in the refrigerator for 24 hours.

3 Cover the dish with foil and cook in a pre-heated oven, 160°C/325°F for 15 minutes. Set aside to cool, then cover and chill thoroughly.

4 Cook the potatoes in boiling salted water for 10–15 minutes, until just tender, then drain. While still warm, cut into large dice and place in a bowl. Combine the French dressing and mayonnaise, add to the potatoes while warm and toss evenly. Leave until cold, then sprinkle the potato salad with chopped spring onions.

5 Place the fish on serving plates and pour a little of the juices over each portion of fish. Garnish with salad leaves and serve immediately with the potato salad.

lobster salad & lime dressing

ingredients

SERVES 4

450 g/1 lb waxy potatoes, scrubbed and sliced

150 ml/5 fl oz mayonnaise

2 tbsp lime juice

finely grated rind of 1 lime

1 tbsp chopped fresh parsley

2 tbsp olive oil

225 g/8 oz cooked lobster meat, removed from the shell and separated into large pieces

2 tomatoes, deseeded and diced

2 hard-boiled eggs, quartered

1 tbsp pitted green olives, quartered

salt and pepper

method

1 Cook the potatoes in a saucepan of boiling water for 10–15 minutes, or until cooked through. Drain well and set aside.

2 In a medium bowl, combine the mayonnaise, 1 tbsp of the lime juice, half the grated lime rind and half the chopped parsley. Set aside.

3 In a separate bowl, whisk the remaining lime juice with the olive oil and pour the dressing over the potatoes.

4 Arrange the potatoes on a serving plate. Top with the lobster meat, tomatoes, eggs and olives. Season to taste with salt and pepper and sprinkle with the reserved parsley. Spoon the mayonnaise onto the centre of the salad. Top with the reserved rind and serve.

light meals

When you need to think of something light and delicious to eat for lunch or supper, potatoes are the answer. It's always a good idea to keep a few generously proportioned old potatoes on hand – you can simply rinse and dry them, prick them all over with a fork, brush with a little vegetable oil, sprinkle with sea salt, pop them in the oven, then forget about them until they are ready to be removed an hour or so later, crisp and golden brown on the outside and meltingly soft on the inside. To make a baked potato really special, mash the flesh with some tasty additions, spoon it back into the skins, and return to the oven to brown. Wonderful! Try using sweet potatoes to ring the changes, or use a mashed potato mixture to stuff mushrooms.

Potatoes are the basis for fishcakes, fritters and croquettes – cooked, mashed and cooled, they mix readily with fish or meat, vegetables and seasonings, and are easily moulded for coating and frying. Very simple potato cakes are lovely served with bacon and maple syrup – a great brunch dish for lazy days.

When you have a little time to spare, try a variation on the classic pasta ravioli – plump, golden potato parcels stuffed with a ground beef filling. Or another Italian favourite, Potato and Spinach Gnocchi – lots of nutrition in one small package!

potato cakes

ingredients

SERVES 8–10

550 g/1 lb 4 oz floury
   potatoes, peeled and
   cut into chunks
salt and pepper
25 g/1 oz butter,
   plus extra to serve
1 egg (optional)
115 g/4 oz plain flour

method

1 To make the mashed potato, cook the potatoes in a large saucepan of boiling salted water for 15–20 minutes. Drain well and mash with a potato masher until smooth. Season to taste with salt and pepper and add the butter. Mix in the egg, if using.

2 Turn the mixture out into a large mixing bowl and add enough of the flour to make a light dough. Work quickly as you do not want the potato to cool too much.

3 Place the dough on a lightly floured work surface and roll out carefully to a thickness of 5 mm/1/4 inch. Using a 6-cm/2 1/2-inch pastry cutter, cut the dough into circles.

4 Heat a greased frying pan. Cook the potato cakes in batches for 4–5 minutes on each side until they are golden brown.

5 Keep warm on a hot plate and serve at once with lots of fresh butter.

feta & potato cakes

ingredients

SERVES 4

500 g/1 lb 2 oz floury
    potatoes, unpeeled

salt and pepper

4 spring onions, chopped

115 g/4 oz feta cheese,
    crumbled

2 tsp chopped fresh thyme

1 egg, beaten

1 tbsp lemon juice

plain flour, for dusting

3 tbsp corn oil

fresh chives, to garnish

method

1 Cook the potatoes in lightly salted boiling water for about 25 minutes, or until tender. Drain and peel. Place the potatoes in a bowl and mash well with a potato masher or fork.

2 Add the spring onions, feta, thyme, egg and lemon juice and season to taste with salt and pepper. Mix thoroughly. Cover the bowl with clingfilm and chill in the refrigerator for 1 hour.

3 Take small handfuls of the potato mixture and roll into balls about the size of a walnut between the palms of your hands. Flatten each one slightly and dust all over with flour. Heat the oil in a frying pan over high heat and cook the potato cakes, in batches if necessary, until golden brown on both sides. Drain on kitchen paper and serve, garnished with the fresh chives.

feta & spinach omelette

ingredients

SERVES 4

6 tbsp butter

1.3 kg/3 lb diced
waxy potatoes

3 garlic cloves, crushed

1 tsp paprika

2 tomatoes, skinned,
deseeded, and diced

12 eggs

pepper

filling

225 g/8 oz baby spinach

1 tsp fennel seeds

125 g/4$^{1}/_{2}$ oz feta cheese,
diced

4 tbsp plain yogurt

method

1 Heat 2 tablespoons of the butter in a frying pan and cook the potatoes over low heat, stirring constantly, for 7–10 minutes, until golden. Transfer to a bowl.

2 Add the garlic, paprika and tomatoes to the frying pan and cook for 2 minutes.

3 Whisk the eggs together and season with pepper. Pour the eggs into the potatoes and mix well.

4 Cook the spinach for 1 minute in boiling water, until just wilted. Drain and refresh under cold running water. Pat dry with kitchen paper. Stir in the fennel seeds, feta cheese and yogurt.

5 Heat a quarter of the remaining butter in a 15-cm/6-inch omelette pan. Ladle a quarter of the egg and potato mixture into the pan. Cook, turning once, for 2 minutes, until set.

6 Transfer the omelette to a serving plate. Spoon a quarter of the spinach mixture onto one half of the omelette, fold the omelette in half over the filling. Repeat to make a further 3 omelettes, then serve.

sweet potato blinis

ingredients

SERVES 4

115 g/4 oz sweet potatoes,
    peeled and cut into chunks

pepper

1 tsp ground allspice

55 g/2 oz wholewheat flour

1 egg

150 ml/5 fl oz skimmed milk

1 egg white

filling

85 g/3 oz prosciutto,
    fat discarded

3 tomatoes, thickly sliced

115 g/4 oz cream cheese

1 tbsp finely grated lemon rind

1 tbsp chopped fresh parsley

25 g/1 oz rocket leaves

method

1 Cook the sweet potatoes in boiling water over medium heat for 15 minutes, or until soft. Drain and mash until smooth, then season with pepper to taste and stir in the ground allspice and flour. Place in a mixing bowl.

2 Add the whole egg and beat it into the mashed sweet potatoes, then gradually stir in the milk to give a thick batter consistency. Set aside until required.

3 To prepare the filling, first preheat the grill. Cut the prosciutto into strips. Place the tomatoes on a foil-lined grill rack and, just before serving, cook under the preheated hot grill for 3–4 minutes or until hot. Blend the cream cheese with the lemon rind and parsley. Set aside.

4 Whisk the egg white until stiff and stir it into the sweet potato batter. Heat a non-stick frying pan until hot, then place 3–4 spoonfuls of the batter in the frying pan and swirl to form a 7.5-cm/3-inch circle. Cook for 2–3 minutes, or until set, then turn over and cook for a further 2–3 minutes, or until golden. Keep warm while you cook the remaining batter.

5 Place 2–3 blinis on a plate and top with a little rocket, prosciutto and grilled tomato slices, then spoon over a little of the cream cheese and serve.

pan potato cake

ingredients

SERVES 4

675 g/1 lb 8 oz waxy
    potatoes, unpeeled and
    sliced

1 carrot, diced

225 g/8 oz small
    broccoli florets

5 tbsp butter

2 tbsp vegetable oil

1 red onion, cut into quarters

2 garlic cloves, crushed

175 g/6 oz firm tofu, drained
    and diced

2 tbsp chopped fresh sage

75 g/2¾ oz grated Cheddar
    cheese

method

1 Cook the sliced potatoes in a large saucepan of boiling water for 10 minutes, then drain thoroughly and set aside.

2 Cook the carrot and broccoli florets in a separate saucepan of boiling water for 5 minutes. Drain with a slotted spoon.

3 Heat the butter and oil in a 2-cm/9-inch frying pan. Add the onion and garlic and cook over low heat for 2–3 minutes. Add half of the potato slices to the frying pan, covering the base of the pan. Cover the potato slices with the carrot, broccoli and tofu. Sprinkle with half of the sage and cover with the remaining potato slices. Sprinkle the grated cheese over the top.

4 Cook over moderate heat for 8–10 minutes, then place the pan under a preheated medium grill for 2–3 minutes, or until the cheese melts and browns.

5 Garnish with the remaining chopped sage and serve immediately.

rösti with roasted vegetables

ingredients

SERVES 4

900 g/2 lb potatoes,
    halved if large
salt and pepper
corn oil, for cooking

pesto dressing

2 tbsp pesto
1 tbsp boiling water
1 tbsp extra-virgin olive oil

roasted vegetables

2 tbsp extra-virgin olive oil
1 tbsp balsamic vinegar
1 tsp honey
1 red pepper, deseeded
    and quartered
2 courgettes, sliced
    lengthways
2 red onions, quartered
1 small fennel bulb,
    cut into thin wedges
16 vine-ripened tomatoes
8 garlic cloves
2 fresh rosemary sprigs

method

1 For the roasted vegetables, mix together the oil, vinegar and honey in a large, shallow dish. Add the red pepper, courgettes, onions, fennel, tomatoes, garlic and rosemary and toss in the marinade. Marinate for 1 hour.

2 Cook the potatoes in a saucepan of lightly salted boiling water for 8–10 minutes, or until partially cooked. Cool, then coarsely grate.

3 Transfer the vegetables, except the tomatoes and garlic, and the marinade to a roasting tin. Roast in a preheated oven, 200°C/400°F, for 25 minutes, then add the tomatoes and garlic and roast for a further 15 minutes, or until the vegetables are tender and slightly blackened around the edges.

4 Meanwhile, cook the rösti. Take a quarter of the potato mixture in your hands and form into a roughly shaped cake. Heat just enough oil to cover the bottom of a frying pan over medium heat. Put the cakes, 2 at a time, into the frying pan and flatten with a spatula to form circles about 2 cm/3/4 inch thick.

5 Cook the rösti for 6 minutes on each side, or until golden brown and crisp. Mix the dressing ingredients. To serve, top each rösti with the roasted vegetables and drizzle with a little pesto dressing. Season to taste.

vegetable rösti

ingredients

SERVES 4

1 carrot, grated

1 courgette, grated

1 sweet potato, grated

8 spring onions, finely
    chopped or shredded

pepper

1 egg white, beaten

2 tsp extra-virgin olive oil

8 lean bacon slices, to serve
    (optional)

method

1 Mix all the vegetables together and season with pepper to taste, then stir in the egg white. Using clean hands, form into 8 small cakes. Press them firmly together.

2 Heat the oil in a non-stick frying pan and cook the cakes over gentle heat for 5–6 minutes, or until golden. Turn over halfway through the cooking time and press down with the back of a spatula. Do this in 2 batches to prevent the frying pan from being overcrowded.

3 Meanwhile, preheat the grill and line the grill rack with foil. Place the bacon under the grill and cook for 5-8 minutes, until crisp. Turn the slices over halfway through the cooking time.

4 As soon as the cakes and bacon are cooked, serve immediately.

potato ravioli

ingredients

SERVES 4

filling

1 tbsp vegetable oil

125 g/4^1/$_2$ oz minced beef

1 shallot, diced

1 garlic clove, crushed

1 tbsp plain flour

1 tbsp tomato purée

150 ml/5 fl oz beef stock

1 celery stalk, chopped

2 tomatoes, skinned and diced

2 tsp chopped fresh basil

salt and pepper

ravioli

450 g/1 lb diced floury
    potatoes

3 medium egg yolks

3 tbsp olive oil

salt and pepper

175 g/6 oz plain flour, plus
    extra for dusting

5 tbsp butter, for frying

shredded basil leaves,
    to garnish

method

1 To make the filling, heat the oil in a saucepan and cook the beef for 3–4 minutes, breaking it up with a spoon. Add the shallot and garlic and cook for 2–3 minutes, until the shallot has softened. Stir in the flour and tomato purée and cook for 1 minute. Stir in the stock, celery, tomatoes and the chopped fresh basil. Season to taste with salt and pepper. Cook the mixture over low heat for 20 minutes. Remove from the heat and cool.

2 To make the ravioli, cook the potatoes in a saucepan of boiling water for 10 minutes, until tender. Mash the potatoes in a mixing bowl. Add the egg yolks and oil. Season, then stir in the flour and mix to form a dough.

3 On a lightly floured surface, divide the dough into 24 pieces and shape into flat circles. Spoon the filling onto one half of each circle and fold the dough over to encase the filling, pressing down to seal the edges.

4 Melt the butter in a frying pan and cook the ravioli, in batches, for 6–8 minutes, turning once, until golden. Serve hot, garnished with shredded basil leaves.

potato & spinach gnocchi

ingredients

SERVES 4

300 g/10^1/$_2$ oz diced floury
    potatoes
175 g/6 oz spinach
1 egg yolk
1 tsp olive oil
125 g/4^1/$_2$ oz plain flour
salt and pepper
spinach leaves, to garnish

sauce

1 tbsp olive oil
2 shallots, chopped
1 garlic clove, crushed
300 ml/10 fl oz passata
2 tsp soft light brown sugar

method

1 Cook the diced potatoes in a saucepan of boiling water for 10 minutes, or until cooked through. Drain and mash the potatoes.

2 Meanwhile, in a separate saucepan, blanch the spinach in a little boiling water for 1–2 minutes. Drain and shred the leaves.

3 Transfer the mashed potato to a lightly floured cutting board and make a well in the centre. Add the egg yolk, olive oil, spinach and a little of the flour. Quickly mix the ingredients into the potato, adding more flour as you go, to make a smooth, firm dough. Divide the mixture into very small dumplings.

4 Cook the gnocchi, in batches, in a saucepan of lightly salted, boiling water for about 5 minutes or until they rise to the surface.

5 Meanwhile, make the sauce. Put the oil, shallots, garlic, passata and sugar into a saucepan and cook over low heat for 10–15 minutes or until the sauce has thickened and reduced.

6 Drain the gnocchi using a slotted spoon and transfer to warm serving dishes. Spoon the sauce over the gnocchi and garnish with the fresh spinach leaves.

baked potatoes with pesto

ingredients

SERVES 4

4 baking potatoes,
    about 225 g/8 oz each

salt and pepper

150 ml/5 fl oz double cream

150 ml/5 fl oz vegetable stock

1 tbsp lemon juice

2 garlic cloves, crushed

3 tbsp chopped basil

2 tbsp pine nuts

2 tbsp grated Parmesan cheese

method

1 Scrub the potatoes well and prick the skins with a fork. Rub a little salt into the skins and place on a baking tray. Cook in a preheated oven, 190°C/375°F for 1 hour, or until the potatoes are cooked through and the skins are crisp.

2 Remove the potatoes from the oven and cut them in half lengthways. Using a spoon, scoop the potato flesh into a mixing bowl, leaving a thin shell of potato inside the skins. Mash the potato flesh with a fork.

3 Meanwhile, mix the cream and stock in a saucepan and simmer over low heat for about 8–10 minutes, or until reduced by half.

4 Stir in the lemon juice, garlic and chopped basil and season to taste with salt and pepper. Stir the mixture into the mashed potato flesh, together with the pine nuts.

5 Spoon the mixture back into the potato shells and sprinkle the Parmesan cheese on top. Return to the oven for 10 minutes, or until the cheese has browned. Serve.

stuffed baked potatoes

ingredients

SERVES 4

900 g/2 lb baking potatoes,
    scrubbed

2 tbsp vegetable oil

1 tsp coarse sea salt

115 g/4 oz butter

1 small onion, chopped

salt and pepper

115 g/4 oz grated Cheddar
    cheese or crumbled blue
    cheese

snipped fresh chives,
    to garnish

optional

4 tbsp canned, drained
    sweetcorn

4 tbsp cooked mushrooms,
    courgette or peppers

method

1 Prick the potatoes in several places with a fork and put on a baking sheet. Brush with the oil and sprinkle with the salt. Bake in a preheated oven, 190°C/375°F, for 1 hour, or until the skins are crispy and the insides are soft when pierced with a fork.

2 Meanwhile, melt 1 tablespoon of the butter in a small frying pan over low-medium heat. Add the onion and cook, stirring occasionally, for 8–10 minutes until soft and golden. Remove from the heat and set aside.

3 Cut the potatoes in half lengthways. Scoop the flesh into a large bowl, leaving the skins intact. Set aside the skins. Increase the oven temperature to 200°C/400°F.

4 Coarsely mash the potato flesh and mix in the onion and remaining butter. Add salt and pepper to taste and stir in any of the optional ingredients. Spoon the mixture back into the reserved potato skins. Top with the cheese.

5 Cook the filled potato skins in the oven for 10 minutes, or until the cheese has melted and is beginning to brown. Garnish with chives and serve immediately.

sweetcorn & green bean-filled baked sweet potatoes

ingredients

SERVES 4

4 red-fleshed sweet potatoes,
    about 250 g/9 oz each
115 g/4 oz frozen
    broad beans
115 g/4 oz frozen sweetcorn
115 g/4 oz fine long
    green beans
140 g/5 oz tomatoes
1 tbsp olive oil
1 tbsp balsamic vinegar
freshly ground black pepper
2 tbsp torn fresh basil leaves,
    plus extra leaves to garnish

method

1 Scrub the sweet potatoes and pierce the skin of each potato with a sharp knife several times. Arrange on a baking sheet and bake in a preheated oven, 190°C/375°F, for 1–1¹/4 hours or until soft and tender when pierced with the point of a sharp knife. Keep warm.

2 When the potatoes are cooked, bring a saucepan of water to the boil, add the broad beans and sweetcorn, and return to the boil. Reduce the heat, cover and simmer for 5 minutes. Trim the green beans, cut in half and add to the saucepan. Return to the boil, then reduce the heat, cover and simmer for 3 minutes or until the green beans are just tender.

3 Blend the oil with the vinegar in a small bowl and season to taste with pepper. Drain the sweetcorn and beans, return to the pan, add the tomatoes and pour the dressing over. Add the torn basil leaves and mix well.

4 Remove the sweet potatoes from the oven, cut in half lengthways and open up. Divide the sweetcorn and bean filling between the potatoes and serve at once, garnished with basil leaves.

sweet potato & mozzarella salad

ingredients

SERVES 4

2 sweet potatoes, peeled
and cut into chunks

2 tbsp olive oil

pepper

2 garlic cloves, crushed

1 large aubergine, sliced

2 red peppers, deseeded
and sliced

200 g/7 oz mixed salad leaves

2 x 150 g/5^{1}/$_{2}$ oz mozzarella
cheeses, drained and sliced

wholewheat bread, to serve

dressing

1 tbsp balsamic vinegar

1 garlic clove, crushed

3 tbsp olive oil

1 small shallot, finely chopped

2 tbsp chopped mixed fresh
herbs, such as tarragon,
chervil and basil

pepper

method

1 Put the sweet potato chunks into a roasting tin with the oil, pepper to taste and garlic and toss to combine. Roast in a preheated oven, 190°C/375°F, for 30 minutes, or until soft and slightly charred.

2 Meanwhile, preheat the grill to high. Arrange the aubergine and pepper slices on the grill pan and cook under the preheated grill, turning occasionally, for 10 minutes, or until soft and slightly charred.

3 To make the dressing, whisk the balsamic vinegar, garlic and oil together in a small bowl and stir in the shallot and herbs. Season to taste with pepper.

4 To serve, divide the salad leaves between 4 serving plates and arrange the sweet potato, aubergine, peppers and mozzarella on top. Drizzle with the dressing and serve with wholewheat bread.

potato & cauliflower fritters

ingredients

SERVES 4

225 g/8 oz diced floury
    potatoes
225 g/8 oz cauliflower florets
35 g/1¼ oz freshly grated
    Parmesan cheese
salt and pepper
1 egg
1 egg white, for coating
vegetable oil, for deep-frying
paprika, for dusting (optional)
crispy bacon strips, chopped,
    to serve

method

1 Cook the potatoes in a saucepan of boiling water for about 10 minutes, until cooked through. Drain well and mash with a fork or potato masher.

2 Meanwhile, cook the cauliflower florets in a separate saucepan of boiling water for 10 minutes. Drain thoroughly and gently mix into the mashed potato. Stir in the grated Parmesan cheese and season to taste.

3 Separate the whole egg and beat the yolk into the potato and cauliflower, mixing well. Lightly whisk both the egg whites in a clean bowl, then carefully fold into the potato and cauliflower mixture.

4 Divide the potato mixture into 8 equal portions and shape them into circles. Pour the oil in a frying pan until half full, then heat it until hot. Cook the fritters for 3–5 minutes, turning once halfway through cooking.

5 Dust the fritters with a little paprika, if you like, and serve with the crispy chopped bacon.

thai potato stir-fry

ingredients

SERVES 4

900 g/2 lb waxy potatoes, cut
    into small dice

2 tbsp vegetable oil

1 yellow pepper, deseeded
    and diced

1 red pepper, deseeded
    and diced

1 carrot, cut into thin strips

1 courgette, cut into thin
    strips

2 garlic cloves, crushed

1 red chilli, sliced

1 bunch spring onions,
    halved lengthways

125 ml/4 fl oz
    coconut milk

1 tsp chopped lemon grass

2 tsp lime juice

finely grated zest of 1 lime

1 tbsp chopped fresh
    coriander

method

1 Bring a large saucepan of water to the boil
and cook the diced potatoes for 5 minutes.
Drain thoroughly.

2 Heat the vegetable oil in a wok or large frying
pan, swirling the oil around the base of the
wok until it is really hot.

3 Add the potatoes, peppers, carrot, courgette,
garlic, and chilli to the wok, and
stir-fry the vegetables for 2–3 minutes.

4 Stir in the spring onions, coconut milk,
chopped lemon grass, and lime juice, and stir-
fry the mixture for a further 2 minutes. Add
the lime zest and coriander and stir-fry for 1
minute. Serve hot.

creamy stuffed mushrooms

ingredients

SERVES 4

25 g/1 oz dried ceps

225 g/8 oz diced floury
    potatoes

salt and pepper

2 tbsp butter, melted

4 tbsp double cream

2 tbsp chopped fresh chives

8 large open-cup mushrooms

25 g/1 oz grated Emmenthal
    cheese

150 ml/5 fl oz vegetable stock

fresh chives, to garnish

method

1 Place the dried ceps in a small bowl. Add sufficient boiling water to cover and soak for 20 minutes, then drain and chop finely.

2 Cook the potatoes in a medium saucepan of lightly salted, boiling water for 10 minutes, until cooked through and tender. Drain well and mash until smooth with a fork or potato masher. Mix in the chopped ceps.

3 Blend together the butter, cream and chopped chives and pour into the ceps and potato mixture, mixing well. Season to taste with salt and pepper.

4 Remove the stems from the open-cup mushrooms. Chop the stems and stir them into the potato mixture. Spoon the mixture into the open-cup mushrooms and sprinkle the cheese over the top. Arrange the filled mushrooms in a shallow ovenproof dish and pour in the vegetable stock.

5 Cover the dish and cook in a preheated oven, 220°C/425°F, for 20 minutes. Remove the lid and cook for 5 minutes, until golden. Serve the mushrooms immediately, garnished with the fresh chives.

potato cakes with bacon & maple syrup

ingredients

SERVES 4

115 g/4 oz cold mashed
  potatoes
225 ml/8 fl oz milk
75 g/2¾ oz self-raising flour
pinch of salt
1 egg, beaten
corn oil, for cooking

to serve

8 good-quality bacon rashers,
  broiled until crisp
1½ tbsp maple syrup

method

1 Blend the mashed potatoes and milk in a food processor or blender to a thin purée.

2 Sift the flour and salt into a mixing bowl, make a well in the centre of the flour, and add the beaten egg and potato purée. Using a balloon whisk, gradually mix the flour into the liquid ingredients, whisking well to make a smooth, creamy, fairly thick batter.

3 Heat a little oil in a large, non-stick frying pan. Pour a small ladleful of batter per cake into the frying pan – you will probably fit about 3 in the frying pan at one time. Cook each cake for 2 minutes on each side until golden brown. Remove from the frying pan and keep warm while you cook the remaining potato cakes.

4 Divide the cakes between 4 warmed plates, top each serving with 2 bacon rashers, and drizzle with maple syrup.

croquettes with ham

ingredients

SERVES 4

450 g/1 lb diced floury
    potatoes
300 ml/10 fl oz milk
2 tbsp butter
4 spring onions, chopped
75 g/2³/4 oz grated Cheddar
    cheese
50 g/1³/4 oz chopped smoked
    ham
1 celery stalk, diced
1 egg, beaten
5 tbsp plain flour
vegetable oil, for deep-frying
salt and pepper
tomato and cucumber
    wedges, to garnish

coating
2 eggs, beaten
125 g/4¹/2 oz fresh whole
    wheat breadcrumbs

sauce
2 tbsp butter
2 tbsp plain flour
150 ml/5 fl oz milk
150 ml/5 fl oz vegetable stock
75 g/2³/4 oz grated Cheddar
    cheese
1 tsp Dijon mustard
1 tbsp chopped fresh
    coriander

method

1 Place the potatoes in a saucepan with the milk and bring to the boil. Reduce to a simmer until the liquid has been absorbed and the potatoes are cooked through and tender.

2 Add the butter and mash the potatoes. Stir in the spring onions, cheese, ham, celery, egg and flour. Season and leave to cool.

3 To make the coating, whisk the eggs in a bowl. Put the breadcrumbs in a separate bowl. Shape the potato mixture into 8 balls. First dip them in the egg, then coat in the breadcrumbs.

4 To make the sauce, melt the butter in a saucepan. Add the flour and cook for 1 minute. Remove from the heat and stir in the milk, stock, cheese, mustard, and coriander. Bring to the boil, stirring until thickened. Reduce the heat and keep the sauce warm, stirring occasionally.

5 In a deep-fat fryer, heat the oil to 180–190°C/350–375°F and fry the croquettes, in batches, for about 5 minutes, until golden. Drain well, garnish with tomato and cucumber wedges, and serve with the sauce.

potato & pepperoni pizza

ingredients

SERVES 4

1 tbsp butter, plus extra
    for greasing
plain flour, for dusting
900 g/2 lb diced floury
    potatoes
2 garlic cloves, crushed
2 tbsp chopped mixed
    fresh herbs
1 egg, beaten
6 tbsp passata
2 tbsp tomato purée
50 g/1³/₄ oz pepperoni slices
1 green pepper, deseeded
    and cut into strips
1 yellow pepper, deseeded
    and cut into strips
2 large open-cup
    mushrooms, sliced
25 g/1 oz pitted black olives,
    cut into quarters
125 g/4¹/₂ oz mozzarella
    cheese, sliced

method

1 Grease and flour a 23-cm/9-inch pizza pan. Cook the potatoes in a saucepan of boiling water for about 10 minutes, until cooked through. Drain and mash until smooth. Transfer to a bowl and stir in the butter, garlic, herbs and egg.

2 Spread the mixture into the prepared pizza pan. Cook in a preheated oven, 220°C/425°F, for 7–10 minutes, or until the pizza base begins to set.

3 Combine the passata and tomato purée and spoon it over the pizza base, to within 1-cm/¹/₂-inch of the edge of the base. Arrange the pepperoni, peppers, mushrooms and olives on top of the tomatoes.

4 Sprinkle the mozzarella cheese on top of the pizza. Return to the oven for 20 minutes, or until the base is cooked through and the cheese has melted on top. Serve hot.

chicken & banana cakes

ingredients

SERVES 4

450 g/1 lb diced floury
    potatoes
225 g/8 oz chicken mince
1 large banana
2 tbsp plain flour
1 tsp lemon juice
1 onion, chopped finely
2 tbsp chopped fresh sage
salt and pepper
2 tbsp butter
2 tbsp vegetable oil
150 ml/5 fl oz single cream
150 ml/5 fl oz chicken stock
fresh sage leaves, to garnish

method

1 Cook the diced potatoes in a saucepan of boiling water for 10 minutes, until cooked through. Drain and mash the potatoes until they are smooth. Stir in the chicken.

2 Mash the banana and add it to the potatoes with the flour, lemon juice, onion and half of the chopped sage. Season to taste with salt and pepper and stir the mixture together. Divide into 8 equal portions and, with lightly floured hands, shape each portion into a round patty.

3 Heat the butter and oil in a frying pan. Add the potato cakes and cook for 12–15 minutes, or until cooked through, turning once. Remove from the frying pan and keep warm. Stir in the cream and stock with the remaining sage. Cook gently over low heat for 2–3 minutes.

4 Arrange the potato cakes on a serving plate. Garnish with fresh sage leaves and serve with the cream and sage sauce.

deep-fried fish balls with aïoli

ingredients

SERVES 4

650 g/1 lb 7 oz floury potatoes, roughly chopped

650 g/1 lb 7 oz cod or haddock fillets

1 egg yolk, beaten

2 garlic cloves, very finely chopped

2 tbsp chopped fresh parsley

1 tbsp chopped fresh dill

salt and pepper

plain flour, for dusting

corn oil, for deep-frying

fresh watercress or rocket, to garnish

aïoli

1 large egg yolk, at room temperature

1 tbsp white wine vinegar or lemon juice

2 large garlic cloves, peeled

salt and pepper

5 tbsp Spanish extra-virgin olive oil

5 tbsp corn oil

method

1 Cook the potatoes in lightly salted boiling water for 20 minutes, until tender. Place the fish in a saucepan, cover with water, and poach for 8 minutes, or until flaking.

2 To make the aïoli, whisk together the egg yolks, garlic and salt until thick. Whisk in a little olive oil, then a little lemon juice. Continue, adding the oil and lemon juice alternately, until thick and smooth. Cover and set aside.

3 Transfer the fish to a board. Discard the skin and any pin bones. Flake the flesh. Drain the potatoes. Mash with the egg yolk and garlic. Stir in the herbs, then fold in the fish and season to taste with salt and pepper. With floured hands, shape into 20 balls.

4 Heat the oil in a saucepan or deep-fryer to 180–190°C/350–375°F, or until a cube of bread browns in 30 seconds. Deep-fry the balls, in batches, for 2–3 minutes, or until golden brown. Drain on kitchen paper. Garnish with watercress or rocket and serve with the aïoli.

salt cod fritters

ingredients

MAKES 18

450 g/1 lb salt cod

350 g/12 oz floury baking
    potatoes

olive oil, for deep-frying

1 onion, very finely chopped

1 garlic clove, crushed

4 tbsp very finely chopped
    fresh parsley or coriander

1 tbsp capers in brine,
    drained and chopped
    finely (optional)

salt and pepper

1 medium egg, lightly beaten

chopped fresh parsley,
    to garnish

aïoli, to serve (see page 134)

method

1 Break the salt cod into pieces and place in a bowl. Add enough water to cover and stand for 48 hours, changing the water 4 times. Drain, then cook in boiling water for 20–25 minutes, until tender. Drain, then remove all the skin and bones. Using a fork, flake the fish into fine pieces that still retain some texture.

2 Boil the potatoes in their skins until tender. Drain and peel the potatoes, then mash in a large bowl. Set aside.

3 Heat 1 tablespoon of oil in a frying pan. Add the onion and garlic and cook for 5 minutes, stirring frequently, until tender but not brown. Remove with a slotted spoon and drain on kitchen paper.

4 Stir the salt cod, onion and garlic into the mashed potatoes. Stir in the chopped parsley or coriander, and the capers if using. Season generously with pepper. Stir in the beaten egg. Cover with clingfilm and chill for 30 minutes, then adjust the seasoning.

5 Heat 5 cm/2 inches oil in a frying pan to 180–190°C/350–375°F. Drop tablespoonfuls of the salt cod mixture, in batches of 6, into the oil and cook for about 8 minutes, or until golden brown and set. Drain the fritters on kitchen paper. Serve at once, garnished with the parsley, with aïoli for dipping.

fishcakes

ingredients

SERVES 4

450 g/1 lb floury potatoes,
    peeled and cut
    into chunks
450 g/1 lb mixed fish fillets,
    such as cod and salmon,
    skinned
2 tbsp chopped fresh tarragon
grated rind of 1 lemon
2 tbsp double cream
salt and pepper
1 tbsp plain flour
1 egg, beaten
115 g/4 oz breadcrumbs,
    made from day-old white
    or wholewheat bread
4 tbsp vegetable oil, for frying
watercress salad, to serve

method

1 Cook the potatoes in a large saucepan of boiling salted water for 15–20 minutes. Drain thoroughly and mash with a potato masher until smooth.

2 Place the fish in a frying pan and just cover with water. Over a medium heat bring to the boil, then reduce the heat, cover and simmer gently for 5 minutes until cooked. Remove from the heat and drain the fish onto a plate. When cool enough to handle, flake the fish roughly into good-sized pieces, ensuring that there are no bones.

3 Mix the potato with the fish, tarragon, lemon rind and cream. Season well with salt and pepper, then shape into 4 round cakes or 8 smaller ones. Dust the cakes with flour and dip them into the beaten egg. Coat thoroughly in the breadcrumbs. Place on a baking tray and chill for at least 30 minutes.

4 Heat the oil in the frying pan and cook the cakes over medium heat for 5 minutes on each side, turning them carefully using a palette knife or a fish slice.

5 Serve with a crisp watercress salad.

tuna fishcakes

ingredients

SERVES 4

225 g/8 oz potatoes, diced
1 tbsp olive oil
1 large shallot, chopped finely
1 garlic clove, chopped finely
1 tsp fresh thyme leaves
400 g/14 oz canned tuna
  in olive oil, drained
grated rind $1/2$ lemon
1 tbsp chopped fresh parsley
salt and pepper
2–3 tbsp plain flour
1 egg, lightly beaten
115 g/4 oz fresh
  breadcrumbs
vegetable oil, for shallow frying
salad, to serve

quick tomato sauce

2 tbsp olive oil
400 g/14 oz canned
  chopped tomatoes
1 garlic clove, crushed
1 tsp sugar
grated rind 1 lemon
1 tbsp chopped fresh basil
salt and pepper

method

1 For the tuna fishcakes, cook the potatoes in plenty of boiling salted water for 12–15 minutes, until tender. Mash, leaving a few lumps, and set aside. Heat the oil in a small frying pan and cook the shallot gently for 5 minutes, until softened. Add the garlic and thyme leaves and cook for 1 minute more. Cool slightly, then add to the potatoes with the tuna, lemon rind and parsley. Season to taste with salt and pepper. Mix together well, but leave some texture.

2 Form the mixture into 6–8 cakes. Dip the fishcakes first in the flour, then the egg and finally the breadcrumbs, to coat. Chill in the refrigerator for 30 minutes.

3 Meanwhile, make the tomato sauce. Put all the ingredients into a saucepan and bring to the boil. Cover and simmer gently for 30 minutes. Uncover and simmer for a further 15 minutes, until thickened and reduced.

4 Heat enough oil in a frying pan to cover the base generously. When hot, add the chilled fishcakes, in batches, and cook for 3–4 minutes on each side, until golden and crisp. Drain on kitchen paper while you cook the remaining fishcakes. Serve hot with the tomato sauce and salad.

tuna & cheese quiche

ingredients

SERVES 4

shell

450 g/1 lb diced floury
    potatoes

2 tbsp butter

6 tbsp plain flour,
    plus extra for dusting

mixed vegetables or salad,
    to serve

filling

1 tbsp vegetable oil

1 shallot, chopped

1 garlic clove, crushed

1 red pepper, deseeded
    and diced

175 g/6 oz canned tuna in
    brine, drained

50 g/1¾ oz canned
    sweetcorn, drained

150 ml/5 fl oz skimmed milk

3 eggs, beaten

1 tbsp chopped fresh dill

salt and pepper

50 g/1¾ oz grated Cheddar
    cheese

fresh dill sprigs and
    lemon wedges, to garnish

method

1 Cook the potatoes in a saucepan of boiling water for 10 minutes, or until tender. Drain and mash the potatoes. Add the butter and flour and mix to form a dough.

2 Knead the potato dough on a floured work surface and press the mixture into a 20-cm/8-inch flan tin. Prick the base with a fork. Line with baking parchment and baking beans and bake blind in a preheated oven, 200°C/400°F, for 20 minutes.

3 Heat the oil in a frying pan. Cook the shallot, garlic and pepper for 5 minutes. Spoon the mixture into the flan shell. Flake the tuna and arrange it on top with the sweetcorn.

4 In a bowl, combine the milk, eggs and dill and season with salt and pepper. Pour the mixture into the flan shell and sprinkle the grated cheese on top.

5 Bake in the oven for 20 minutes, or until the filling has set. Garnish the flan with fresh dill and lemon wedges. Serve with mixed vegetables or salad.

main meals

When it comes to main meals that will fill you and warm you when the weather is not at its best, potatoes definitely have the edge. Potato-topped pies, baked in the oven until they are golden brown and crisp, simply thrill the senses – they smell wonderful, look gorgeous and taste … well, try for yourself. Fisherman's Pie is definitely one to start with – it manages to be homely and elegant at the same time. Carrot-topped Beef Pie also has a mashed-potato topping, with carrot added, or for a meatless version, try Potato-topped Vegetables.

Pastry-topped pies are also very welcoming – Potato, Beef and Kidney Pie is a variation on the steak and kidney pudding. Potato, Leek and Chicken Pie has a flaky filo pastry topping, while Parathas and Curry Pies enfold a spicy potato filling.

Casseroles are always a winner – Stifado is a beef casserole made in every Greek kitchen, and the French Country Casserole, made with lamb, is especially good with a flavouring of mint and a touch of rosé wine!

For another touch of sophistication, try Potato, Fontina and Rosemary Tart – sitting on a puff pastry base, it really is irresistible. The Potato, Herb and Smoked Salmon Gratin is quite wonderful, too, and very chic – serve this when you want to impress!

potato, fontina & rosemary tart

ingredients

SERVES 4

1 quantity puff pastry

plain flour, for dusting

filling

3–4 waxy potatoes, peeled

300 g/10½ oz fontina cheese, cut into cubes

1 red onion, thinly sliced

3 large fresh rosemary sprigs

2 tbsp olive oil

1 egg yolk

salt and pepper

method

1 Roll out the pastry on a lightly floured work surface into a circle about 25 cm/10 inches in diameter and put on a baking sheet.

2 Slice the potatoes as thinly as possible so that they are almost transparent – use a mandolin if you have one. Arrange the potato slices in a spiral, overlapping the slices to cover the pastry, leaving a 2-cm/¾-inch margin around the edge.

3 Arrange the cheese and onion over the potatoes, sprinkle with the rosemary and drizzle over the oil. Season to taste with salt and pepper and brush the edges with the egg yolk to glaze.

4 Bake in a preheated oven, 190°C/375°F, for 25 minutes, or until the potatoes are tender and the pastry is brown and crisp. Serve hot.

tomato & potato tortilla

ingredients

SERVES 6

1 kg/2 lb 4 oz potatoes,
    peeled and cut into
    small cubes
salt and pepper
2 tbsp olive oil
1 bunch of spring onions,
    chopped
115 g/4 oz cherry tomatoes
6 eggs
3 tbsp water
2 tbsp chopped fresh parsley

method

1 Cook the potatoes in a saucepan of lightly salted boiling water for 8–10 minutes, or until tender. Drain and set aside until required.

2 Preheat the grill to medium. Heat the oil in a large frying pan. Add the spring onions and cook until just softened. Add the potatoes and cook for 3–4 minutes, until coated with oil and hot. Smooth the top and sprinkle the tomatoes throughout.

3 Mix the eggs, water, salt and pepper and parsley in a bowl, then pour into the frying pan. Cook over very gentle heat for 10–15 minutes, until the tortilla looks fairly set.

4 Place the frying pan under the hot grill and cook until the top is brown and set. Cool for 10–15 minutes before sliding out of the frying pan onto a cutting board. Cut into wedges and serve at once.

vegetable and potato-topped pie

ingredients

SERVES 2

500 g/1 lb 2 oz potatoes, cut into chunks
2 tbsp semi-skimmed milk
1 tsp olive oil
1 small onion, peeled and finely chopped
55 g/2 oz dried brown lentils
1 garlic clove, peeled and chopped
1 celery stalk, trimmed and finely chopped
115 g/4 oz finely chopped brown-cap mushrooms
1 medium carrot, peeled and finely chopped
125 ml/4 fl oz vegetable stock
2 tsp Worcestershire sauce
400 g/14 oz canned chopped tomatoes with herbs
1 tsp dried mixed herbs
pepper
25 g/1 oz grated Cheddar cheese

method

1 Put the potatoes in a saucepan with water to cover and bring to the boil, then simmer for 15 minutes, or until tender. Drain and mash the potatoes with the milk. Set aside.

2 While the potatoes are cooking, heat the oil in a non-stick frying pan and sauté the onion over medium heat for a few minutes, stirring occasionally, to soften.

3 Add the lentils, garlic and celery to the frying pan and stir, then add the mushrooms, carrot, stock, Worcestershire sauce, tomatoes and herbs and stir everything well to combine. Bring to a simmer, then cover and cook gently for 25 minutes, or until the sauce is thick and the lentils are tender. If the mixture looks too dry during cooking, add a little more stock or water. Taste and season with pepper if necessary.

4 Spoon the lentil mixture into a baking dish and level the top. Spoon over the mashed potato and sprinkle with the cheese.

5 Bake in a preheated oven, 190°C/375°F, for 15 minutes, or until the potatoes are golden.

potato & broccoli pie

ingredients

SERVES 4

450 g/1 lb waxy potatoes,
    cut into chunks
2 tbsp butter
1 tbsp vegetable oil
175 g/6 oz lean pork, diced
1 red onion, cut into 8 wedges
2¹/₂ tbsp plain flour, plus
    extra for dusting
150 ml/5 fl oz vegetable stock
150 ml/5 fl oz milk
75 g/2³/₄ oz dolcelatte
    cheese, crumbled
75 g/2³/₄ oz broccoli florets
25 g/1 oz walnuts
salt and pepper
225 g/8 oz ready-made puff
    pastry, thawed if frozen
milk, for glazing

method

1 Cook the potato chunks in a saucepan of boiling water for 5 minutes, then drain and set aside.

2 Meanwhile, heat the butter and oil in a heavy saucepan. Add the pork and cook for 5 minutes, turning frequently, until browned.

3 Add the onion and cook for 2 minutes more. Stir in the flour and cook for 1 minute, then gradually stir in the vegetable stock and milk. Bring to the boil, stirring constantly.

4 Add the dolcelatte, broccoli florets, potatoes and walnuts to the pan and simmer for 5 minutes. Season with salt and pepper to taste, then spoon the mixture into a pie dish.

5 On a floured work surface, roll out the puff pastry until it is 2.5 cm/1 inch larger than the dish. Cut a 2.5-cm/1-inch wide strip from the pastry. Dampen the edge of the dish and place the pastry strip around it. Brush with milk and put the pastry lid on top.

6 Seal and crimp the edges and make 2 small slits in the centre of the lid. Brush with milk and cook in a preheated oven, 200°C/400°F, for 25 minutes, or until the pastry has risen and is golden.

potato-topped vegetables

ingredients

SERVES 4

1 carrot, diced

175 g/6 oz cauliflower florets

175 g/6 oz broccoli florets

1 fennel bulb, sliced

75 g/2¾ oz green beans, halved

2 tbsp butter

2½ tbsp plain flour

150 ml/5 fl oz vegetable stock

150 ml/5 fl oz dry white wine

150 ml/5 fl oz milk

175 g/6 oz crimini mushrooms, cut into quarters

2 tbsp chopped fresh sage

topping

900 g/2 lb diced floury potatoes

2 tbsp butter

4 tbsp plain yogurt

75 g/2¾ oz freshly grated Parmesan cheese

1 tsp fennel seeds

salt and pepper

method

1 Cook the carrot, cauliflower, broccoli, fennel and beans in a large saucepan of boiling water for 10 minutes, until just tender. Drain the vegetables thoroughly and set aside.

2 Melt the butter in a saucepan. Stir in the flour and cook for 1 minute. Remove from the heat and stir in the stock, wine and milk. Return to the heat and bring to the boil, stirring until thickened. Stir in the reserved vegetables, mushrooms and sage.

3 Meanwhile, make the topping. Cook the diced potatoes in a saucepan of boiling water for 10–15 minutes. Drain and mash with the butter, yogurt and half the Parmesan cheese. Stir in the fennel seeds and season to taste.

4 Spoon the vegetable mixture into a 1-litre/1¾ pint pie dish. Spoon the potato over the top and sprinkle with the remaining cheese. Cook in a preheated oven, 190°C/375°F, for 30–35 minutes, until golden.

vegetable-stuffed parathas

ingredients

SERVES 6

pastry

225 g/8 oz wholewheat flour
(ata or chapati flour), plus
extra for dusting

1/2 tsp salt

200 ml/7 fl oz water

about 4 tbsp vegetable ghee

filling

675 g/1 lb 8 oz potatoes

1/2 tsp ground turmeric

1 tsp garam masala

1 tsp finely chopped fresh
root ginger

1 tbsp chopped fresh
coriander leaves

3 fresh green chillies,
deseeded and finely
chopped

1 tsp salt

method

1 To make the parathas, combine the flour, salt, water and 1 1/4 teaspoons of the ghee in a bowl to form a dough.

2 Divide the dough into 6 equal portions. Roll each portion out on a floured work surface. Brush the middle of each of the dough portions with 1/2 teaspoon of the remaining ghee. Fold the dough portions in half and roll into a pipelike shape, then flatten with the palms of your hands, and roll around a finger to form a coil. Roll out again, using flour to dust when necessary, to form a circle 18 cm/ 7 inches in diameter.

3 To make the filling, place the potatoes in a large saucepan of boiling water and cook until soft enough to be mashed.

4 Blend the turmeric, garam masala, ginger, coriander leaves, chillies and salt together in a bowl. Add the spice mixture to the mashed potato and mix well. Spread about 1 tablespoon of the spicy potato mixture on each dough portion and cover with another rolled-out piece of dough. Seal the edges well.

5 Heat 2 teaspoons of the remaining ghee in a heavy frying pan. Place the parathas gently in the pan, in batches, and cook, turning and moving them about gently with a flat spoon, until golden. Remove the parathas from the pan and serve immediately.

curry pies

ingredients

SERVES 4

225 g/8 oz plain
   wholewheat flour
100 g/3$^{1}/_{2}$ oz margarine, cut
   into small pieces
4 tbsp water
2 tbsp oil
225 g/8 oz diced root
   vegetables, such as
   potatoes, carrots
   and parsnips
1 small onion, chopped
2 garlic cloves, finely chopped
$^{1}/_{2}$ tsp curry powder
$^{1}/_{2}$ tsp ground turmeric
$^{1}/_{2}$ tsp ground cumin
$^{1}/_{2}$ tsp wholegrain mustard
5 tbsp vegetable stock
soy milk, to glaze

method

1 Place the flour in a mixing bowl and rub in the margarine with your fingertips until the mixture resembles breadcrumbs. Stir in the water and bring together to form a soft dough. Wrap and chill in the refrigerator for 30 minutes.

2 To make the filling, heat the oil in a large saucepan. Add the diced root vegetables, chopped onion and garlic and cook, stirring occasionally, for 2 minutes. Stir in the spices and the mustard, turning the vegetables to coat them thoroughly. Cook the vegetables, stirring constantly, for another minute.

3 Add the stock to the saucepan and bring to the boil. Cover and simmer, stirring occasionally, for about 20 minutes, until the vegetables are tender and the liquid has been absorbed. Set aside to cool.

4 Divide the dough into 4 portions. Roll each portion into a 15-cm/6-inch circle. Place the filling on one half of each circle.

5 Brush the edges of each circle with soy milk, then fold over, and press the edges firmly together to seal. Place on a baking sheet. Bake in a preheated oven, 200°C/400°F, for 25–30 minutes, until golden brown.

sweet potato curry with lentils

ingredients

SERVES 1

1 tsp vegetable oil

100 g/3^1/$_2$ oz sweet potato, peeled and cut into bite-size cubes

75 g/2^3/$_4$ oz potato, cut into bite-size cubes

1 small onion, peeled and finely chopped

1 small garlic clove, peeled and finely chopped

1 small fresh green chilli, deseeded and chopped

^{1}/$_2$ tsp ground ginger

55 g/2 oz dried green lentils

75–100 ml hot vegetable stock

pepper

^{1}/$_2$ tsp garam masala

1 tbsp low-fat plain yogurt

basmati rice, boiled, to serve

method

1 Heat the oil in a non-stick, lidded saucepan and sauté the sweet potato over medium heat, turning occasionally, for 5 minutes.

2 Meanwhile, bring the potato cubes to the boil in a saucepan of water, then simmer until almost cooked (about 6 minutes). Drain and set aside.

3 Remove the sautéed sweet potato cubes with a slotted spoon. Add the onion to the saucepan and cook, stirring occasionally, for 5 minutes, or until transparent. Add the garlic, chilli and ginger and stir for 1 minute.

4 Return the sweet potato to the saucepan with the boiled potato and the lentils, half the stock, pepper to taste and garam masala. Stir to combine, bring to a simmer, and cover. Reduce the heat and simmer gently for 20 minutes, adding a little more stock if the curry looks too dry.

5 Stir in the yogurt and serve with boiled basmati rice.

cauliflower gratin

ingredients

SERVES 4

500 g/1 lb 2 oz cauliflower
   florets
600 g/1 lb 5 oz potatoes,
   diced
100 g/3^1/$_2$ oz cherry tomatoes

sauce

2 tbsp butter or margarine
1 leek, sliced
1 garlic clove, crushed
3 tbsp plain flour
300 ml/10 fl oz milk
75 g/2^3/$_4$ oz mixed grated
   cheese, such as mature
   Cheddar, Parmesan
   and Gruyère cheese
^{1}/$_2$ tsp paprika
2 tbsp chopped fresh
   flat-leaf parsley
salt and pepper
chopped fresh parsley,
   to garnish

method

1 Cook the cauliflower and potatoes in separate pans of boiling water for 10 minutes. Drain and set aside.

2 To make the sauce, melt the butter or margarine in a saucepan and sauté the leek and garlic for 1 minute. Stir in the flour and cook, stirring constantly, for 1 minute. Remove the saucepan from the heat and gradually stir in the milk, 55 g/2 oz of the cheese, the paprika and the parsley. Return the pan to the heat and bring to the boil, stirring constantly. Season with salt and pepper to taste.

3 Spoon the cauliflower into a deep ovenproof dish. Add the cherry tomatoes and top with the potatoes. Pour the sauce over the potatoes and sprinkle on the remaining cheese.

4 Cook in a preheated oven, 180°C/350°F, for 20 minutes, or until the vegetables are cooked through and the cheese is golden brown and bubbling. Garnish with parsley and serve immediately.

spanish potatoes

ingredients

SERVES 4

675 g/1 lb 8 oz diced waxy
     potatoes
3 tbsp olive oil
1 onion, halved and sliced
2 garlic cloves, crushed
400 g/14 oz canned plum
     tomatoes, chopped
75 g/2^3/$_4$ oz chorizo
     sausage, sliced
1 green pepper, deseeded
     and cut into strips
^{1}/$_2$ tsp paprika
25 g/1 oz pitted black olives,
     halved
8 eggs
salt and pepper
1 tbsp chopped fresh parsley
crusty bread, to serve

method

1 Cook the diced potatoes in a saucepan of boiling water for 10 minutes, or until softened. Drain thoroughly and set aside.

2 Heat the olive oil in a large frying pan. Add the sliced onion and garlic and cook gently for 2–3 minutes, until the onion softens.

3 Add the chopped canned tomatoes and cook over low heat for about 10 minutes, until the mixture has reduced slightly.

4 Stir the potatoes into the saucepan with the chorizo, green pepper, paprika and olives. Season to taste with salt and pepper. Cook for 5 minutes, stirring. Transfer to a shallow ovenproof dish.

5 Make 8 small hollows in the top of the mixture with the back of a spoon and carefully break an egg into each hollow. Season the eggs with salt and pepper. Cook in a preheated oven, 220°C/425°F, for 5–6 minutes, or until the eggs are just cooked.

6 Sprinkle the potatoes with chopped parsley and serve immediately with crusty bread.

layered cheese & potatoes

ingredients

SERVES 4

900 g/2 lb unpeeled waxy
  potatoes, cut into wedges

2 tbsp butter

1 red onion, halved and sliced

2 garlic cloves, crushed

2^1/$_2$ tbsp plain flour

600 ml/1 pint milk

400 g/14 oz canned artichoke
  hearts in brine, drained
  and halved

150 g/5^1/$_2$ oz frozen mixed
  vegetables, thawed

125 g/4^1/$_2$ oz grated Gruyère
  cheese

125 g/4^1/$_2$ oz grated Cheddar
  cheese

50 g/1^3/$_4$ oz crumbled
  Gorgonzola

25 g/1 oz freshly grated
  Parmesan cheese

225 g/8 oz firm tofu, drained
  and sliced

2 tbsp chopped fresh thyme

salt and pepper

fresh thyme sprigs, to garnish

method

1 Cook the potato wedges in a saucepan of boiling water for 10 minutes. Drain thoroughly.

2 Meanwhile, melt the butter in a saucepan. Add the sliced onion and garlic and cook over low heat, stirring frequently, for 2–3 minutes. Stir the flour into the pan and cook, stirring, for 1 minute. Gradually add the milk and bring to the boil, stirring constantly.

3 Reduce the heat and add the artichoke hearts, mixed vegetables, half of each of the 4 cheeses and the tofu to the pan, mixing well. Stir in the chopped thyme and season with salt and pepper to taste.

4 Arrange a layer of parboiled potato wedges in the base of a shallow ovenproof dish. Spoon the vegetable mixture over the top and cover with the remaining potato wedges. Sprinkle the rest of the 4 cheeses over the top.

5 Cook in a preheated oven, 200°C/400°F, for 30 minutes, or until the potatoes are cooked and the top is golden brown. Serve garnished with fresh thyme sprigs.

roasted ratatouille & potato wedges

ingredients

SERVES 4

300 g/10^1/$_2$ oz potatoes in
  their skins, scrubbed
200 g/7 oz aubergine, cut into
  1-cm/^{1}/$_2$-inch wedges
125 g/4^1/$_2$ oz red onion cut
  into 5-mm/^{1}/$_4$-inch slices
200 g/7 oz deseeded mixed
  peppers, sliced into
  1-cm/^{1}/$_2$-inch strips
175 g/6 oz courgette, cut in
  half lengthways, then into
  1-cm/^{1}/$_2$-inch slices
125 g/4^1/$_2$ oz cherry tomatoes
90 g/3^1/$_4$ oz fromage frais
1 tsp runny honey
pinch of smoked paprika
1 tsp chopped fresh parsley

marinade
1 tsp vegetable oil
1 tbsp lemon juice
4 tbsp white wine
1 tsp sugar
2 tbsp chopped fresh basil
1 tsp finely chopped fresh
  rosemary
1 tbsp finely chopped fresh
  lemon thyme
^{1}/$_4$ tsp smoked paprika

method

1 Bake the potatoes in a preheated oven, 200°C/400°F, for 30 minutes, then remove and cut into wedges – the flesh should not be completely cooked.

2 To make the marinade, place all the ingredients in a bowl and blend with a hand-held electric blender until smooth, or use a food processor.

3 Put the potato wedges into a large bowl with the aubergine, onion, peppers and courgette, then pour over the marinade and mix well.

4 Arrange the vegetables on a non-stick baking tray and roast in the oven, turning occasionally, for 25–30 minutes, or until golden brown and tender. Add the tomatoes for the last 5 minutes of the cooking time just to split the skins and warm slightly.

5 Mix the fromage frais, honey and paprika together in a bowl.

6 Serve the vegetables with the fromage frais mixture, and sprinkled with chopped parsley.

beef en daube
with mustard mash

ingredients

SERVES 2

2 tsp vegetable oil

225 g/8 oz extra-lean braising
    steak, cut into 8 pieces

10 small shallots, peeled but
    left whole

1 garlic clove, peeled
    and crushed

1 medium tomato, chopped

225 g/8 oz finely sliced
    mushrooms

150 ml/5 fl oz red wine

100 ml/4 fl oz chicken stock

1 small bouquet garni

pepper

1 tsp cornflour

mustard mash

2 medium floury potatoes,
    peeled and sliced

25 ml/³/₄ fl oz milk, heated

1 tsp Dijon mustard, to taste

method

1 Heat the oil in a heavy-based flameproof casserole. Add the meat and shallots and cook over high heat, stirring, for 4–5 minutes to brown the meat on all sides. Add the garlic, tomato, mushrooms, wine and stock and tuck the bouquet garni well in.

2 Bring to a simmer on the stove, then cover and transfer to a preheated oven, 180°C/350°F, to cook for 45–60 minutes, or until everything is tender.

3 About 30 minutes before the beef is ready, place the potatoes in boiling water and simmer for 20 minutes, or until just tender. Remove from the heat, then drain well and put in a bowl. Add the milk and mash well. Stir in the mustard to taste and keep warm.

4 Use a slotted spoon to remove the meat and vegetables to a warmed serving dish. Cook the sauce over high heat until reduced by half. Reduce the heat, then remove the bouquet garni and check the seasoning.

5 Mix the cornflour with a little cold water to form a paste. Add to the sauce, stirring well, and bring back to a simmer. Pour the sauce over the meat and serve with the mustard mash.

stifado

ingredients

SERVES 6

450 g/1 lb tomatoes, peeled
150 ml/5 fl oz beef stock
2 tbsp olive oil
450 g/1 lb shallots, peeled
2 garlic cloves, finely chopped
700 g/1 lb 9 oz stewing steak,
    cut into 2.5-cm/1-inch
    cubes
1 fresh rosemary sprig
1 bay leaf
2 tbsp red wine vinegar
salt and pepper
450 g/1 lb potatoes,
    cut into quarters

method

1 Place the tomatoes in a blender or food processor, add the stock and process to a purée. Alternatively, push them through a sieve into a bowl with the back of a wooden spoon and mix with the stock.

2 Heat the oil in a large, heavy-based saucepan. Add the shallots and garlic and cook over low heat, stirring occasionally, for 8 minutes, or until golden. Transfer to a plate with a perforated spoon. Add the steak to the pan and cook, stirring frequently, for 5–8 minutes, or until browned.

3 Return the shallots and garlic to the pan, add the tomato mixture, herbs and vinegar and season to taste with salt and pepper. Cover and simmer gently for 1^1/$_2$ hours. Add the potatoes, re-cover, and simmer for a further 30 minutes. Remove and discard the rosemary and bay leaf and serve at once.

carrot-topped beef pie

ingredients

SERVES 4

450 g/1 lb lean minced beef
1 onion, chopped
1 garlic clove, crushed
1 tbsp plain flour
300 ml/10 fl oz beef stock
2 tbsp tomato purée
1 celery stalk, chopped
3 tbsp chopped fresh parsley
1 tbsp Worcestershire sauce
salt and pepper
675 g/1 lb 8 oz floury diced
    potatoes
2 large carrots, diced
2 tbsp butter
3 tbsp skimmed milk

method

1 Dry-fry the beef in a large saucepan over high heat for 3–4 minutes, or until sealed. Add the onion and garlic and cook for 5 minutes more, stirring. Add the flour and cook for 1 minute.

2 Gradually blend in the beef stock and tomato purée. Stir in the celery, 1 tablespoon of the parsley, and the Worcestershire sauce. Season to taste with salt and pepper. Bring the mixture to the boil, then reduce the heat, and simmer for 20–25 minutes. Spoon the mixture into a 1.25-litre/2^{1}/4-pint pie dish.

3 Meanwhile, cook the potatoes and carrots in a pan of boiling water for 10 minutes. Drain thoroughly and mash them together.

4 Stir the butter, milk and the remaining parsley into the potato and carrot mixture, and season with salt and pepper to taste. Spoon the potato on top of the beef mixture to cover it completely; alternatively, pipe the potato on top with a pastry bag.

5 Cook in a preheated oven, 190°C/375°F, for 45 minutes, or until cooked through. Serve piping hot.

potato, beef & kidney pie

ingredients

SERVES 4

225 g/8 oz waxy potatoes,
diced

2 tbsp butter

450 g/1 lb lean steak, diced

150 g/5$\frac{1}{2}$ oz ox kidney,
cored and chopped

12 shallots

2$\frac{1}{2}$ tbsp plain flour, plus
extra for dusting

150 ml/5 fl oz beef stock

150 ml/5 fl oz light ale

salt and pepper

225 g/8 oz ready-made puff
pastry, thawed if frozen

1 egg, beaten

method

1 Cook the diced potatoes in a saucepan of boiling water for 10 minutes. Drain thoroughly.

2 Meanwhile, melt the butter in a saucepan and add the diced steak and the kidney. Cook over medium heat for 5 minutes, stirring until the meat is sealed on all sides. Add the shallots and cook for 3–4 minutes more. Stir in the flour and cook for 1 minute. Gradually stir in the beef stock and light ale and bring to the boil, stirring constantly.

3 Stir the potatoes into the meat mixture and season to taste with salt and pepper. Reduce the heat until the mixture is just simmering gently. Cover the pan and cook for 1 hour, stirring occasionally. Spoon the beef mixture into the base of a pie dish.

4 Roll out the pastry on a lightly floured work surface to an oval 1-cm/$\frac{1}{2}$-inch larger than the top of the dish. Cut a strip of pastry long enough and wide enough to fit around the edge of the dish. Brush the edge of the dish with beaten egg and press the pastry strip around the edge. Brush with egg and place the pastry lid on top. Crimp to seal the edge and then knock up the edge with the back of a knife blade. Brush with beaten egg to glaze.

5 Cook in a preheated oven, 230°C/450°F, for 20–25 minutes, or until the pastry has risen and is golden brown. Serve immediately.

french country casserole

ingredients

SERVES 6

2 tbsp corn oil

2 kg/4 lb 8 oz boneless leg of
    lamb, cut into 2.5-cm/
    1-inch cubes

6 leeks, sliced

1 tbsp plain flour

150 ml/5 fl oz rosé wine

300 ml/10 fl oz chicken stock

1 tbsp tomato purée

1 tbsp sugar

2 tbsp chopped fresh mint

115 g/4 oz dried apricots,
    chopped

salt and pepper

1 kg/2 lb 4 oz potatoes, sliced

3 tbsp melted unsalted butter

fresh mint sprigs, to garnish

method

1 Heat the oil in a large, flameproof casserole. Cook the lamb in batches over medium heat, stirring, for 5–8 minutes, or until browned. Transfer to a plate.

2 Add the sliced leeks to the casserole and cook, stirring occasionally, for 5 minutes, or until softened. Sprinkle in the flour and cook, stirring, for 1 minute. Pour in the wine and stock and bring to the boil, stirring. Stir in the tomato purée, sugar, chopped mint and apricots and season to taste.

3 Return the lamb to the casserole and stir. Arrange the potato slices on top and brush with the melted butter. Cover and bake in a preheated oven, 180°C/350°F, for 1 1/2 hours.

4 Increase the oven temperature to 200°C/ 400°F, uncover the casserole and bake for a further 30 minutes, or until the potato topping is golden brown. Serve immediately, garnished with fresh mint sprigs.

potato, leek & chicken pie

ingredients

SERVES 4

225 g/8 oz waxy potatoes, diced

5 tbsp butter

1 skinless, boneless chicken breast portion, about 175 g/6 oz, diced

1 leek, sliced

150 g/5¹/₂ oz crimini mushrooms, sliced

2¹/₂ tbsp plain flour

300 ml/10 fl oz milk

1 tbsp Dijon mustard

2 tbsp chopped fresh sage

salt and pepper

225 g/8 oz filo pastry, thawed if frozen

3 tbsp butter, melted

method

1 Cook the diced potatoes in a saucepan of boiling water for 5 minutes. Drain and set aside.

2 Melt the butter in a frying pan and cook the chicken for 5 minutes, or until browned all over. Add the leek and mushrooms and cook over medium heat, stirring occasionally, for 3 minutes. Stir in the flour and cook, stirring constantly, for 1 minute. Gradually add the milk and bring to the boil. Add the mustard, chopped sage and potatoes, season and then simmer the mixture for 10 minutes.

3 Meanwhile, line a deep pie dish with half of the sheets of filo pastry. Spoon the sauce into the dish and cover with one sheet of pastry. Brush the pastry with butter and lay another sheet on top. Brush this sheet with butter.

4 Cut the remaining filo pastry into strips and fold them onto the top of the pie to create an attractive, ruffled effect. Brush the strips with the remaining melted butter and cook the pie in a preheated oven, 180°C/350°F, for 45 minutes, or until golden brown and crisp. Serve hot.

quick baked chicken

ingredients

SERVES 4

500 g/1 lb 2 oz minced
    chicken

1 large onion, chopped finely

2 carrots, chopped finely

2 tbsp plain flour

1 tbsp tomato purée

300 ml/10 fl oz chicken stock

salt and pepper

pinch of fresh thyme

1.5 kg/3 lb 5 oz mashed
    potatoes, creamed with
    butter and milk and
    well seasoned

75 g/2¾ oz grated Cheddar
    cheese

cooked peas, to serve

method

1 Brown the minced chicken, onion and carrots in a non-stick saucepan for 5 minutes, stirring frequently. Sprinkle the chicken with the flour and cook over low heat for a further 2 minutes.

2 Gradually blend in the tomato purée and chicken stock, then simmer for 15 minutes. Season to taste with salt and pepper and add a pinch of fresh thyme. Transfer to a casserole and cool slightly.

3 Spoon the mashed potato over the chicken mixture and sprinkle with cheese. Bake in a preheated oven, 200°C/400°F, for 20 minutes, or until the cheese is bubbling and golden.

4 Serve straight from the casserole, with peas.

potato & turkey pie

ingredients

SERVES 4

300 g/10¹/₂ oz waxy potatoes, diced
2 tbsp butter
1 tbsp vegetable oil
300 g/10¹/₂ oz lean turkey meat, diced
1 red onion, halved and sliced
2 tbsp plain flour, plus extra for dusting
300 ml/10 fl oz milk
150 ml/5 fl oz double cream
2 celery stalks, sliced
75 g/2³/₄ oz dried apricots, chopped
25 g/1 oz walnut pieces
2 tbsp chopped fresh parsley
salt and pepper
225 g/8 oz ready-made unsweetened shortcrust pastry, thawed if frozen
beaten egg, for brushing

method

1 Place the diced potatoes in a saucepan of boiling water and cook for 10 minutes, until tender. Drain and set aside.

2 Meanwhile, heat the butter and oil in a heavy saucepan. Add the diced turkey and cook over medium heat, stirring frequently, for 5 minutes, until golden brown.

3 Add the sliced onion and cook for 2–3 minutes. Stir in the flour and cook, stirring constantly, for 1 minute. Gradually stir in the milk and cream. Bring to the boil, stirring, then lower the heat to a simmer.

4 Stir in the celery, apricots, walnut pieces, parsley and potatoes. Season to taste with salt and pepper. Spoon the potato and turkey mixture into the base of a 1.25-litre/2¹/₄-pint pie dish.

5 On a lightly floured work surface, roll out the pastry to 2.5-cm/1-inch larger than the dish. Trim a 2.5-cm/1-inch wide strip and place it on the dampened rim of the dish. Brush with water and cover with the pastry lid.

6 Brush the top of the pie with beaten egg to glaze and cook in a preheated oven, 200°C/400°F, for 25–30 minutes, or until the pie is cooked and golden brown. Serve immediately.

potato, herb & smoked salmon gratin

ingredients

SERVES 6

400 ml/14 fl oz milk

3 whole cloves

2 bay leaves

50 g/1^3/$_4$ oz onion, sliced

85 g/3 oz leek, chopped

100 g/3^1/$_2$ oz lightly cured smoked salmon, finely sliced into strips

350 g/12 oz potatoes, cut into 2-mm/^{1}/$_{16}$-inch slices

2 tbsp finely chopped fresh chives

2 tbsp finely chopped fresh dill

1 tbsp finely chopped fresh tarragon

2 tsp wholegrain mustard

pepper

35 g/1^1/$_4$ oz watercress

method

1 Pour the milk into a large, heavy-based saucepan, add the cloves, bay leaves, onion, leek and smoked salmon and heat over low heat. When the milk is just about to reach simmering point, carefully remove the smoked salmon with a slotted spoon and cool on a plate.

2 Add the potatoes to the milk and stir with a wooden spoon. Return to a simmer and cook, stirring occasionally to prevent the potatoes from sticking, for 12 minutes, or until the potatoes are just beginning to soften and the milk has thickened slightly from the potato starch. Remove the cloves and bay leaves.

3 Add the herbs, mustard and pepper and stir well. Pour the mixture into a greased and base-lined 19-cm/7^1/$_2$-inch shallow cake tin. Cover with a layer of greaseproof paper and then foil and bake in a preheated oven, 200°C/400°F, for 30 minutes.

4 Remove from the oven and place a pan on top. Cool for 20 minutes before turning out onto a baking sheet. Put under a preheated hot grill to brown the top.

5 Cut the gratin into 6 wedges and serve with the smoked salmon, tossed with watercress.

layered fish & potato pie

ingredients

SERVES 4

900 g/2 lb waxy potatoes,
    sliced

5 tbsp butter

1 red onion, halved and sliced

5 tbsp plain flour

450 ml/16 fl oz milk

150 ml/5 fl oz double cream

225 g/8 oz smoked haddock
    fillet, skinned and diced

225 g/8 oz cod fillet,
    skinned and diced

1 red pepper, deseeded
    and diced

125 g/4^1/$_2$ oz broccoli florets

salt and pepper

50 g/1^3/$_4$ oz freshly grated
    Parmesan cheese

method

1 Cook the sliced potatoes in a saucepan of boiling water for 10 minutes. Drain well and set aside.

2 Meanwhile, melt the butter in a saucepan, then add the onion and cook gently for 3–4 minutes. Add the flour and cook for 1 minute. Blend in the milk and cream and bring to the boil, stirring until the sauce has thickened.

3 Arrange about half of the potato slices in the base of a shallow, ovenproof dish. Add the fish, diced pepper and broccoli to the sauce and cook over low heat for 10 minutes. Season with salt and pepper, then spoon the mixture over the potatoes in the dish.

4 Arrange the remaining potato slices in a layer over the fish mixture. Sprinkle the Parmesan cheese over the top. Cook in a preheated oven, 180°C/350°F, for 30 minutes, or until the topping is golden.

fisherman's pie

ingredients

SERVES 6

110 g/3½ oz butter, plus
extra for greasing

900 g/2 lb white fish fillets,
such as plaice, skinned

salt and pepper

150 ml/5 fl oz dry white wine

1 tbsp chopped fresh parsley,
tarragon or dill

175 g/6 oz small mushrooms,
sliced

175 g/6 oz cooked
peeled prawns

40 g/1½ oz plain flour

125 ml/4 fl oz double cream

900 g/2 lb floury potatoes,
peeled and cut into chunks

method

1 Fold the fish fillets in half and place in a buttered ovenproof dish. Season well with salt and pepper, pour over the wine and scatter over the herbs. Cover with foil and bake in a preheated oven, 180°C/350°F, for 15 minutes until the fish starts to flake. Strain off the liquid and reserve for the sauce. Increase the oven temperature to 220°C/425°F.

2 Sauté the mushrooms in a frying pan with 15 g/½ oz of the butter and spoon over the fish. Scatter over the prawns.

3 Heat 55 g/2 oz of the butter in a saucepan and stir in the flour. Cook for a few minutes without browning, remove from the heat, then add the reserved cooking liquid gradually, stirring well between each addition. Return to the heat and gently bring to the boil, stirring. Add the cream and season to taste with salt and pepper. Pour over the fish in the dish and smooth over the surface.

4 Meanwhile, cook the potatoes in boiling salted water for 15–20 minutes. Drain well and mash with a potato masher until smooth. Season to taste with salt and pepper and add the remaining butter, stirring until melted. Spoon or pipe the potato onto the fish and sauce and bake for 10–15 minutes until golden brown. Serve immediately.

fish turnovers

ingredients

SERVES 4

dough

450 g/1 lb self-raising flour,
plus extra for dusting

pinch of salt

225 g/8 oz butter, diced, plus
extra for greasing

1 egg, lightly beaten

filling

4 tbsp butter

1 small leek, diced

1 small onion, chopped finely

1 carrot, diced

225 g/8 oz potatoes, diced

350 g/12 oz firm white fish
fillet, cut into 2.5-cm/
1-inch pieces

4 tsp white wine vinegar

75 g/2³/₄ oz grated Cheddar
cheese

1 tsp chopped fresh tarragon

salt and pepper

mixed salad leaves and
tomatoes, to serve

method

1 In a large bowl, sift together the flour and salt. Rub in the butter with your fingertips until the mixture resembles coarse breadcrumbs. Add about 3 tablespoons of cold water and bring together to form a dough. Knead briefly until smooth. Wrap in clingfilm and chill in the refrigerator for 30 minutes.

2 Meanwhile, melt half the butter in a large frying pan and add the leek, onion and carrot. Cook over low heat, stirring occasionally, for 7–8 minutes, until the vegetables are softened. Remove from the heat and cool slightly, then put the vegetable mixture into a large mixing bowl and add the potatoes, fish, vinegar, remaining butter, cheese, tarragon and seasoning. Set aside.

3 Roll the pastry out thinly on a lightly floured work surface. Using a pastry cutter, press out 4 x 19-cm/7¹/₂-inch circles. Divide the filling between the 4 circles. Moisten the edges of the pastry and fold over. Pinch to seal. Crimp the edges firmly and place the turnovers on a lightly greased baking sheet. Brush generously with the beaten egg to glaze.

4 Bake in a preheated oven, 200°C/400°F, for 15 minutes. Remove from the oven and brush again with the egg glaze. Return to the oven for 20 minutes. Serve the turnovers hot or cold with mixed salad leaves and tomatoes.

on the side

Potatoes make a superb side dish, and here again their versatility really shows. They love flavourings such as chilli, garlic, herbs and lemon – or try lime for a change. They go beautifully with cheese, too – Parmesan Potatoes, with a topping of crisp bacon, are a protein-packed accompaniment to a simple main dish, while Soufléed Cheesy Potato Fries make a delectable snack with their light, fluffy, Gruyère-cheese coating. A classic French side dish is Potato and Cheese Gratin – thinly sliced waxy potatoes baked in the oven with Gruyère and double cream, and the merest hint of garlic – vegetarians will love this served as a main dish.

The affinity between potatoes and spices is demonstrated in some very tasty dishes to serve with a curry. Do try grinding the seeds to make the spice mix for Spicy Indian Potatoes, rather than using ground spices – the result will be worth it.

Learning to cook Perfect Roast Potatoes is a must, because they are the natural partner to roast meats, and it is very rewarding to master the art so that you get a fabulous result every time. Soggy roast potatoes just don't have the same appeal. The secret of success is really quite simple – give them a good shake to rough up the surface before you put them into the hot fat, and make sure the fat really is hot!

perfect roast potatoes

ingredients

SERVES 6

1.3 kg/3 lb large potatoes,
  such as King Edwards or
  Desirée, peeled and cut
  into even-size chunks
3 tbsp dripping, goose fat,
  duck fat or olive oil
salt

method

1 Cook the potatoes in a large saucepan of lightly salted boiling water over medium heat, covered, for 5–7 minutes. They will still be firm. Remove from the heat. Meanwhile, add the fat to a roasting tin and place in a preheated oven, 220ºC/425ºF.

2 Drain the potatoes well and return them to the pan. Cover with the lid and firmly shake the pan so that the surface of the potatoes is slightly roughened to help give them a much crisper texture.

3 Remove the roasting tin from the oven and carefully tip the potatoes into the hot fat. Baste them to ensure that they are all coated.

4 Roast the potatoes at the top of the oven for 45–50 minutes, turning the potatoes and basting them once, until they are browned all over and thoroughly crisp.

5 Using a slotted spoon, carefully transfer the potatoes from the roasting tin into a warmed serving dish. Sprinkle with a little salt and serve at once.

parmesan potatoes

ingredients

SERVES 4

1.3 kg/3 lb potatoes

salt

50 g/1³/₄ oz grated Parmesan
    cheese

pinch of freshly
    grated nutmeg

1 tbsp chopped fresh parsley

vegetable oil, for roasting

4 smoked bacon slices,
    cut into thin strips

method

1 Cut the potatoes in half lengthways and cook them in a saucepan of lightly salted, boiling water for 10 minutes. Drain them thoroughly.

2 Combine the grated Parmesan cheese, nutmeg and parsley in a shallow bowl. Roll the potato pieces in the cheese mixture to coat them completely. Shake off any excess.

3 Pour a little oil into a roasting tin and heat it in a preheated oven, 200°C/400°F, for 10 minutes. Remove from the oven and place the potatoes in the tin. Return to the oven and cook for 30 minutes, turning once.

4 Remove from the oven and sprinkle the bacon on top of the potatoes. Return to the oven for 15 minutes, or until the potatoes and bacon are cooked. Drain off any excess fat and serve.

chilli roast potatoes

ingredients

SERVES 4

500 g/1 lb 2 oz small new
    potatoes, scrubbed
150 ml/5 fl oz vegetable oil
1 tsp chilli powder
¹/₂ tsp caraway seeds
1 tsp salt
1 tbsp chopped fresh basil

method

1 Cook the potatoes in a saucepan of boiling water for 10 minutes, then drain thoroughly.

2 Pour a little of the oil into a shallow roasting tin to coat the base. Heat the oil in a preheated oven, 200°C/400°F, for 10 minutes. Add the potatoes to the tin and brush them with the hot oil.

3 In a small bowl, combine the chilli powder, caraway seeds and salt. Sprinkle the mixture over the potatoes, turning to coat them all over.

4 Add the remaining oil to the tin and roast in the oven for about 15 minutes, or until the potatoes are cooked through.

5 Using a slotted spoon, remove the potatoes from the oil, draining them thoroughly, and transfer them to a warmed serving dish. Sprinkle the chopped basil over the top and serve immediately.

homemade oven chips

ingredients

SERVES 4

450 g/1 lb large potatoes,
    peeled
2 tbsp sunflower oil
salt and pepper

method

1 Cut the potatoes into thick, even-sized sticks. Rinse them under cold running water and then dry thoroughly on a clean tea towel. Put in a bowl, add the oil and toss together until coated.

2 Spread the chips on a baking sheet and cook in a preheated oven, 200°C/400°F, for 40–45 minutes, turning once, until golden. Add salt and pepper to taste, and serve hot.

pan-fried potatoes
with piquant paprika

ingredients

SERVES 6

3 tsp paprika

1 tsp ground cumin

$1/4$–$1/2$ tsp cayenne pepper

$1/2$ tsp salt

450 g/1 lb small old potatoes, peeled

corn oil, for pan-frying

sprigs of fresh flat-leaved parsley, to garnish

aïoli, to serve (optional, see page 212)

method

1 Put the paprika, cumin, cayenne pepper and salt in a small bowl and mix well together. Set aside.

2 Cut each potato into 8 thick wedges. Pour corn oil into a large, heavy-based frying pan to a depth of about 2.5 cm/1 inch. Heat the oil, then add the potato wedges, preferably in a single layer, and cook gently for 10 minutes, or until golden brown all over, turning from time to time. Remove from the frying pan with a slotted spoon and drain on kitchen paper.

3 Transfer the potato wedges to a large bowl and, while they are still hot, sprinkle with the paprika mixture, then gently toss them together to coat.

4 Turn the potatoes into a large, warmed serving dish and serve hot, garnished with parsley sprigs. Accompany with a bowl of aïoli for dipping, if wished.

souffléed cheesy potato fries

ingredients

SERVES 4

900 g/2 lb potatoes,
    cut into chunks
150 ml/5 fl oz double cream
75 g/2³/₄ oz grated Gruyère
    cheese
pinch of cayenne pepper
salt and pepper
2 egg whites
vegetable oil, for deep-frying
chopped fresh flat-leaved
    parsley and grated
    cheese, to garnish

method

1 Cook the potatoes in a saucepan of lightly salted, boiling water for about 10 minutes. Drain thoroughly and pat dry with absorbent kitchen paper. Set aside until required.

2 Mix the double cream and Gruyère cheese in a large bowl. Stir in the cayenne pepper and season with salt and pepper to taste.

3 Whisk the egg whites until stiff peaks form. Gently fold into the cheese mixture until fully incorporated. Add the cooked potatoes, turning to coat thoroughly in the mixture.

4 In a deep pan, heat the oil to 180–190°C/350–375°F or until a cube of bread browns in 30 seconds. Remove the potatoes from the cheese mixture with a slotted spoon and cook in the oil, in batches if necessary, for 3–4 minutes, or until golden.

5 Transfer the potatoes to a warmed serving dish and garnish with parsley and grated cheese. Serve immediately.

grilled potatoes with lime mayonnaise

ingredients

SERVES 4

450 g/1 lb potatoes, unpeeled and scrubbed

3 tbsp butter, melted

2 tbsp chopped fresh thyme

salt and pepper

paprika, for dusting

lime mayonnaise

150 ml/5 fl oz mayonnaise

2 tsp lime juice

finely grated rind of 1 lime

1 garlic clove, crushed

pinch of paprika

salt and pepper

method

1 Cut the potatoes into 1-cm/$^1/_2$-inch thick slices. Cook in a saucepan of boiling water for 5–7 minutes; they should still be quite firm. Remove the potatoes with a slotted spoon and drain thoroughly. Line a grill pan with foil, then place the potato slices on the foil.

2 Brush the potatoes with the melted butter and sprinkle the chopped thyme on top. Season to taste with salt and pepper. Cook under a preheated medium grill for 10 minutes, turning them over once.

3 Meanwhile, make the lime mayonnaise. Combine the mayonnaise, lime juice, lime rind, garlic, paprika and salt and pepper to taste in a bowl.

4 Dust the hot potato slices with a little paprika and transfer to a warm serving dish. Serve immediately with the bowl of lime mayonnaise for dipping.

garlic potato wedges

ingredients

SERVES 4

3 large baking potatoes,
    scrubbed

4 tbsp olive oil

2 tbsp butter

2 garlic cloves, chopped

1 tbsp chopped fresh rosemary

1 tbsp chopped fresh parsley

1 tbsp chopped fresh thyme

salt and pepper

method

1 Bring a large saucepan of water to the boil. Add the potatoes and parboil them for 10 minutes. Drain the potatoes and refresh under cold water, then drain them again thoroughly.

2 Transfer the potatoes to a cutting board. When the potatoes are cold enough to handle, cut them into thick wedges, but do not peel.

3 Heat the oil and butter in a small saucepan together with the garlic. Cook gently over low heat until the garlic begins to brown, then remove the pan from the heat. Stir in the herbs and season to taste with salt and pepper. Brush the herb mixture all over the potato wedges.

4 Barbecue the potatoes over hot coals or cook under a grill preheated to hot for 10–15 minutes, brushing liberally with any of the remaining herb and butter mixture, until the potato wedges are just tender.

5 Transfer the garlic potato wedges to a warm serving plate to serve.

baby potatoes with aïoli

ingredients

SERVES 6–8

450 g/1 lb baby new potatoes

1 tbsp chopped fresh
   flat-leaved parsley

salt

aïoli

1 large egg yolk,
   at room temperature

1 tbsp white wine vinegar
   or lemon juice

2 large garlic cloves, peeled

salt and pepper

5 tbsp Spanish extra-virgin
   olive oil

5 tbsp corn oil

method

1 To make the aïoli, blend the egg yolk, vinegar, garlic and salt and pepper to taste in a food processor. With the motor still running, very slowly add the olive oil, then the corn oil, drop by drop at first, then, when it starts to thicken, in a slow, steady stream until the sauce is thick and smooth. Alternatively, mix in a bowl with a whisk. Quickly blend in 1 tablespoon water so that the aïoli forms the consistency of sauce.

2 To prepare the potatoes, cut them in half or quarters to make bite-size pieces. If they are very small, you can leave them whole. Put the potatoes in a large saucepan of cold, salted water and bring to the boil. Lower the heat and simmer for 7 minutes, or until just tender. Drain well, then turn out into a large bowl.

3 While the potatoes are still warm, pour over the aïoli sauce, and gently toss the potatoes in it. Stand for about 20 minutes to allow the potatoes to marinate in the sauce.

4 Transfer the potatoes with aïoli to a warmed serving dish, sprinkle over the parsley and salt to taste and serve warm.

pesto potatoes

ingredients

SERVES 4

900 g/2 lb small new potatoes

75 g/2³/₄ oz fresh basil

2 tbsp pine nuts

3 garlic cloves, crushed

salt and pepper

100 ml/3¹/₂ fl oz olive oil

75 g/2³/₄ oz freshly grated
     Parmesan cheese and
     romano cheese, mixed

fresh basil sprigs, to garnish

method

1 Cook the potatoes in a saucepan of salted boiling water for 15 minutes, or until tender. Drain well, transfer to a warm serving dish, and keep warm until required.

2 Meanwhile, put the basil, pine nuts, garlic and a little salt and pepper to taste in a food processor. Blend for 30 seconds, then add the oil gradually, processing until the mixture is smooth.

3 Remove the mixture from the food processor and place in a mixing bowl. Stir in the grated Parmesan and romano cheeses and mix well to combine.

4 Spoon the pesto sauce over the potatoes and toss lightly and carefully so that the potatoes are thoroughly coated. Garnish with fresh basil sprigs and serve immediately.

lemony & herbed potatoes

ingredients

SERVES 4

lemony new potatoes

1 kg/2 lb 4 oz new potatoes

25 g/1 oz butter

1 tbsp finely grated lemon rind

2 tbsp lemon juice

1 tbsp chopped fresh
    dill or chives

salt and pepper

extra chopped fresh dill or
    chives, to garnish

herbed new potatoes

1 kg/2 lb 4 oz new potatoes

3 tbsp light olive oil

1 tbsp white wine vinegar

pinch of dry mustard

pinch of caster sugar

salt and pepper

2 tbsp chopped mixed fresh
    herbs, such as parsley,
    chives, marjoram, basil
    and rosemary

extra chopped fresh mixed
    herbs, to garnish

method

1 For the lemony potatoes, either scrub the potatoes well or remove the skins by scraping them off with the blade of a sharp knife. Cook the potatoes in plenty of lightly salted, boiling water for about 15 minutes, until just tender. Drain and transfer to a serving bowl.

2 While the potatoes are cooking, melt the butter over low heat. Add the lemon rind, lemon juice and herbs. Season with salt and pepper. Pour the lemony butter mixture over the drained potatoes and stir gently to mix. Garnish with extra herbs and serve hot or warm.

3 For the herbed potatoes, prepare and cook the potatoes as described in step 1. Whisk the olive oil, vinegar, mustard, sugar and seasoning together in a small bowl. Add the chopped herbs and mix well.

4 Pour the oil and vinegar mixture over the drained potatoes, stirring to coat evenly. Garnish with extra fresh herbs and serve warm or cold.

perfect mash

ingredients

SERVES 4

900 g/2 lb floury potatoes

55 g/2 oz butter

3 tbsp hot milk

salt and pepper

method

1 Peel the potatoes, placing them in cold water as you prepare the others to prevent them from going brown.

2 Cut the potatoes into even-sized chunks and cook in a large saucepan of boiling salted water over a medium heat, covered, for 20–25 minutes, or until they are tender.

3 Remove the pan from the heat and drain the potatoes. Return the potatoes to the hot pan and mash with a potato masher until smooth. Add the butter and continue to mash until it is all mixed in, then add the hot milk.

4 Taste the mash and season with salt and pepper as necessary. Serve at once.

trio of potato purées

ingredients

SERVES 4

300 g/10¹/₂ oz floury
potatoes, chopped

125 g/4¹/₂ oz swede, chopped

1 carrot, chopped

450 g/1 lb fresh spinach

1 tbsp skimmed milk

1 tbsp butter, plus extra
for greasing

2¹/₂ tbsp plain flour

1 egg

salt and pepper

¹/₄ tsp ground cinnamon

1 tbsp orange juice

¹/₄ tsp grated nutmeg

carrot batons, to garnish

method

1 Cook the potatoes in a saucepan of boiling water for 10 minutes. In separate pans cook the swede and carrot in boiling water for 10 minutes. Blanch the spinach in boiling water for 5 minutes. Drain the vegetables.

2 Add the milk and the tablespoon of butter to the potatoes and mash until smooth with a fork or potato masher. Stir in the flour and egg and season to taste.

3 Divide the potato mixture between 3 medium bowls. Spoon the swede into one bowl and mix thoroughly. Spoon the carrot into the second bowl and mix thoroughly. Spoon the spinach into the third bowl and mix thoroughly.

4 Add the cinnamon to the swede and potato mixture and season to taste. Stir the orange juice into the carrot and potato mixture. Stir the nutmeg into the spinach and potato mixture.

5 Spoon a layer of the swede and potato mixture into 4 lightly greased 150 ml/5 fl oz ramekins and smooth over the top. Cover each with a layer of spinach and potato mixture, then top with the carrot and potato mixture. Cover the ramekins with foil and place in a roasting pan. Half-fill the pan with boiling water and cook in a preheated oven, 180°C/350°F, for 40 minutes, or until set.

6 Turn out onto serving plates. Garnish with the carrot batons and serve immediately.

hot potato cakes

ingredients

SERVES 4

500 g/1 lb 2 oz potatoes,
    peeled and cut into chunks

salt

2 fresh green chillies, seeded
    and finely chopped

1 fresh red chilli, seeded and
    finely chopped

1 tbsp blanched almonds,
    finely chopped

2 tbsp dry unsweetened
    coconut

1 tbsp chopped fresh
    coriander or parsley

2 tbsp plain flour

2.5-cm/1-inch piece fresh
    root ginger, grated or very
    finely chopped

vegetable oil, for deep-frying

mango chutney, to serve

method

1 Cook the potatoes in a large saucepan of lightly salted boiling water for 20–25 minutes, or until tender. Drain well and mash with a fork or potato masher. Tip into a bowl and set aside until cool enough to handle.

2 Stir the chillies, almonds, coconut, coriander, flour and ginger into the mashed potato, mixing well, and season to taste with salt. Shape the mixture into small balls between the palms of your hands and gently flatten into cakes.

3 Heat the oil for deep-frying to 180–190°C/350–375°F, or until a cube of bread dropped in the oil browns in 30 seconds. Deep-fry the cakes, in batches if necessary, for 5 minutes, or until golden. Drain on kitchen paper and serve at once with the chutney.

potato & cheese gratin

ingredients

SERVES 4–6

900 g/2 lb waxy potatoes,
  such as Charlotte, peeled
  and thinly sliced
1 large garlic clove, halved
225 ml/8 fl oz double cream
freshly grated nutmeg
salt and pepper
175 g/6 oz Gruyère cheese,
  finely grated
butter, for greasing and
  dotting over the top

method

1 Put the potato slices in a bowl, cover with cold water and set aside for 5 minutes, then drain well.

2 Meanwhile, rub the bottom and sides of an oval gratin or ovenproof dish with the cut sides of the garlic halves, pressing down firmly to impart the flavour. Lightly grease the sides of the dish with butter.

3 Place the potatoes in a bowl with the cream, and season to taste with freshly grated nutmeg and salt and pepper. Use your hands to mix everything together, then transfer the potatoes to the gratin dish and pour over any cream remaining in the bowl.

4 Sprinkle the cheese over the top and dot with butter. Place the gratin dish on a baking sheet and bake in a preheated oven, 190°C/375°F, for 60–80 minutes, or until the potatoes are tender when pierced with a skewer and the top is golden and bubbling. Let it stand for about 2 minutes, then serve straight from the gratin dish.

pommes anna

ingredients

SERVES 4

675 g/1 lb 8 oz waxy potatoes
5 tbsp butter, melted
4 tbsp chopped mixed herbs
salt and pepper
chopped fresh herbs,
    to garnish

method

1 Slice the potatoes thinly and pat dry with kitchen paper. Arrange a layer of potato slices in a lightly greased shallow ovenproof dish until the base is covered. Brush with a little butter and sprinkle with a quarter of the chopped mixed herbs. Season to taste.

2 Continue layering the potato slices, brushing each layer with melted butter and sprinkling with herbs, until they are all used up.

3 Brush the top layer of potato slices with butter. Cover the dish and cook in a preheated oven, 190°C/375°F, for 1 1/2 hours.

4 Turn out onto a warm ovenproof platter and return to the oven for 25–30 minutes more, until golden brown. Serve, garnished with the chopped herbs.

potatoes à la boulangère

ingredients

SERVES 2

400 g/14 oz potatoes, very
thinly sliced

1 small onion, peeled and
thinly sliced

freshly ground black pepper,
to taste

50 ml/2 fl oz vegetable stock

50 ml/2 fl oz skimmed milk

1 tsp butter

method

1 Layer the potato and onion slices in a shallow, ovenproof dish, seasoning each layer well with pepper.

2 Mix the stock and milk together and pour over the potatoes. Dot the top layer with the butter, then cover with foil and bake in a preheated oven for 30 minutes.

3 Remove the foil and cook for a further 30 minutes, or until the potatoes are cooked.

potatoes with almonds

ingredients

SERVES 4

600 g/1 lb 5 oz potatoes,
    unpeeled and sliced
1 tbsp vegetable oil
1 red onion, halved and
    sliced
1 garlic clove, crushed
50 g/1³/₄ oz almond slivers
¹/₂ tsp ground turmeric
125 g/4¹/₂ oz rocket leaves
300 ml/10 fl oz double cream
salt and pepper

method

1 Cook the sliced potatoes in a saucepan of boiling water for 10 minutes. Drain them thoroughly.

2 Heat the vegetable oil in a heavy frying pan. Add the onion and garlic and cook over medium heat, stirring frequently, for 3–4 minutes.

3 Add the almonds, turmeric and potato slices and cook, stirring constantly, for about 2–3 minutes. Stir in the rocket leaves.

4 Transfer the potato and almond mixture to a shallow ovenproof dish. Pour the double cream evenly over the top and season to taste with salt and pepper.

5 Cook in a preheated oven, 190°C/375°F, for 20 minutes, or until the potatoes are cooked through. Transfer to a warmed serving dish and serve immediately.

spicy indian potatoes

ingredients

SERVES 4

^{1}/$_2$ tsp coriander seeds

1 tsp cumin seeds

4 tbsp vegetable oil

2 cardamom pods

1 tsp grated fresh root ginger

1 fresh red chilli, seeded
    and chopped

1 onion, chopped

2 garlic cloves, crushed

450 g/1 lb new potatoes,
    quartered

150 ml/5 fl oz vegetable stock

675 g/1 lb 8 oz fresh spinach,
    chopped

4 tbsp plain yogurt

salt and pepper

method

1 Grind the coriander and cumin seeds using a pestle and mortar.

2 Heat the oil in a frying pan. Add the ground coriander and cumin seeds to the pan together with the cardamom pods and ginger and cook for about 2 minutes.

3 Add the chopped chilli, onion and garlic to the pan. Cook for a further 2 minutes, stirring frequently.

4 Add the potatoes to the pan, together with the vegetable stock. Cook gently for about 30 minutes, or until the potatoes are cooked through, stirring occasionally. Add the spinach and cook for 5 minutes more.

5 Remove the frying pan from the heat and stir in the yogurt. Season with salt and pepper to taste. Transfer the potatoes and spinach to a serving dish and serve.

curried potato, cauliflower & spinach

ingredients

SERVES 4

2 tbsp olive oil

1 onion, diced

1 tbsp garam masala

$1/2$ tsp ground cumin

1 tsp ground turmeric

400 g/14 oz canned chopped
tomatoes in tomato juice

300 ml/10 fl oz vegetable
stock

450 g/1 lb new potatoes, cut
into chunks

280 g/10 oz cauliflower florets

55 g/2 oz flaked almonds

250 g/9 oz baby spinach
leaves

naan bread, to serve

method

1 Heat the oil in a saucepan over low-medium heat, add the onion and spices and cook, stirring constantly, for 2–3 minutes, taking care not to burn the spices. Add the tomatoes and stock and bring to the boil, then reduce the heat, cover and simmer for 25 minutes.

2 Meanwhile, put the potatoes into a separate saucepan, cover with cold water, and bring to the boil. Reduce the heat, cover and simmer for 15 minutes. Add the cauliflower and return to the boil, then reduce the heat, cover and simmer for a further 10 minutes, or until just tender.

3 Meanwhile, preheat the grill to medium. Spread the almonds out in a single layer on a baking sheet and toast under the grill, turning to brown evenly, for 1–2 minutes – watch constantly because they brown very quickly. Tip into a small dish and set aside.

4 Add the spinach to the potatoes and cauliflower, stir into the water and simmer for 1 minute. Drain the vegetables and return to the pan. Stir in the curried tomato sauce. Transfer to a warmed serving dish, sprinkle over the toasted almonds and serve at once with naan bread.

bombay potatoes

ingredients

SERVES 4

1 kg/2 lb 4 oz waxy potatoes

2 tbsp vegetable ghee

1 tsp panch poran spice mix

3 tsp ground turmeric

2 tbsp tomato purée

300 ml/10 fl oz plain yogurt

salt

chopped fresh coriander,
    to garnish

method

1 Put the whole potatoes into a large saucepan of salted cold water. Bring to the boil, then simmer for about 15 minutes, until the potatoes are just cooked, but not tender.

2 Heat the ghee in a separate saucepan over medium heat and add the panch poran, turmeric, tomato purée, yogurt and salt. Bring to the boil and simmer, uncovered, for 5 minutes.

3 Drain the potatoes and cut each one into 4 pieces. Add the potatoes to the pan, then cover, and cook briefly. Transfer to an ovenproof casserole. Cook in a preheated oven, 180°C/350°F, for about 40 minutes, or until the potatoes are tender and the sauce has thickened a little.

4 Sprinkle with chopped coriander to garnish and serve the Bombay potatoes immediately.

spiced potatoes & spinach

ingredients

SERVES 4

3 tbsp vegetable oil

1 red onion, sliced

2 garlic cloves, crushed

$^{1}/_{2}$ tsp chilli powder

2 tsp ground coriander

1 tsp ground cumin

150 ml/5 fl oz vegetable stock

300 g/10$^{1}/_{2}$ oz potatoes, diced

500 g/1 lb 2 oz baby spinach

salt and pepper

1 fresh red chilli, seeded
    and sliced

method

1 Heat the oil in a heavy frying pan. Add the onion and garlic and sauté over medium heat, stirring occasionally, for 2–3 minutes.

2 Stir in the chilli powder, ground coriander and ground cumin, and cook, stirring constantly, for about 30 seconds.

3 Add the vegetable stock, diced potatoes and spinach, and bring to the boil. Reduce the heat, cover the frying pan, and simmer gently for about 10 minutes, or until the potatoes are cooked right through and tender.

4 Uncover and season to taste with salt and pepper, then add the red chilli and cook for 2–3 minutes. Transfer the spiced potatoes and spinach to a warmed serving dish and serve immediately.